W9-COU-631

SEVEN WONDERS OF THE MILKY WAY

SEVEN WONDERS OF THE MILKY WAY

DAVID A. AGUILAR

VIKING

VIKING
An imprint of Penguin Random House LLC
375 Hudson Street
New York, New York 10014

First published in the United States of America by Viking,
an imprint of Penguin Random House LLC, 2018

LIBRARY OF CONGRESS CATALOGING IN PUBLICATION DATA IS AVAILABLE
ISBN 9780451476869

Manufactured in China

1 3 5 7 9 10 8 6 4 2

Designed by Jim Hoover   Set in Legacy Serif ITC Std

CONTENTS

INTRODUCTION . . . 7

THE GREAT NEBULA IN ORION: Stellar Nursery . . . 17

OMEGA CENTAURI: Oldest Stars in the Milky Way . . . 25

UY SCUTI: Biggest Star in the Milky Way . . . 33

J1407B: Strangest Planet in the Milky Way . . . 41

TRAPPIST-1: Most Earthlike Planets in the Milky Way . . . 49

THE HOURGLASS NEBULA: Most Beautiful Object in the Milky Way . . . 57

TABBY'S STAR: Weirdest Object in the Milky Way . . . 63

OTHER WONDERS TO WONDER ABOUT . . . 71

BEYOND THE MILKY WAY . . . 74

UNDER THE STARS . . . 77

KEEP EXPLORING! . . . 78

ACKNOWLEDGMENTS . . . 79

INDEX . . . 80

INTRODUCTION

STEP OUTSIDE ON a clear, moonless summer night far away from city lights and look up to a sky filled with stars that dazzle like distant diamonds. Straight overhead is a diffuse band of white light called the Milky Way. This is our home in space. Every planet, moon, and star we see, including our sun, is part of the Milky Way galaxy.

The Romans called it *via lactea*, the "roadway of milk." The Pawnee spoke of it as buffalo dust, kicked up in a race between a ghostly horse and a lone buffalo. The Incas envisioned it as a river, the source of all water that rains down, creating a connection between Earth and sky. To the Maori in New Zealand, it was the *waka*, or canoe, of their god Tamarereti. In East Asia, this hazy band of stars was the "Silver River of Heaven." According to a legend of the Khoisan of the Kalahari Desert in Southern Africa, the night sky was dark and starless until a young girl tossed smoldering embers into the sky and created the Milky Way. In many Native American creation stories, the Milky Way represents the "spirits' way" or the path used by departed souls to reach the heavens. My favorite myth comes from the Cherokee, who tell the story of a hungry dog spirit that stole a bag of cornmeal. As the people gave chase, singing and pounding on their drums, the frightened canine thief leaped into the dark night sky, spilling a trail of the precious food behind him. Each grain of cornmeal became a star. This is why Cherokee storytellers call this wondrous path of stars "the place where the dog spirit ran away."

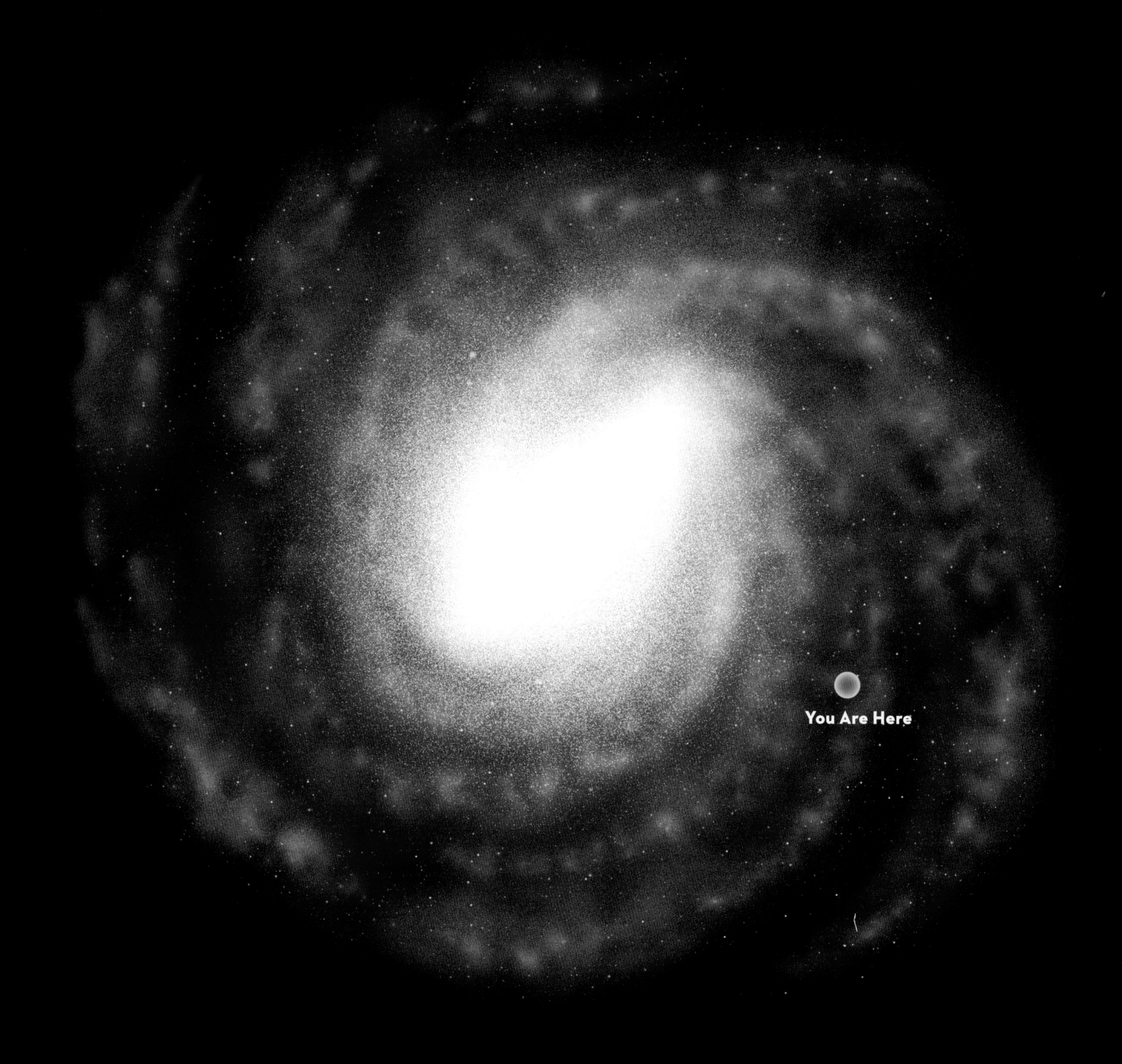
You Are Here

During summer in the northern hemisphere, the bright path of the Milky Way runs south from the constellation Sagittarius the Archer, through Cygnus the Swan, and north to Queen Cassiopeia. It fascinated astronomers like the Italian scientist Galileo Galilei, who in 1610 was the first to point a telescope at the heavens and determine that the Milky Way was an endless expanse of stars invisible to the naked eye.

Fast-forwarding from Galileo's seventeenth century to our twenty-first century, we now know the Milky Way is a collection of billions of stars all moving through space together. And it's just one of *hundreds of billions* of other galaxies out there. Many of them are spiral galaxies like ours, while others are quite different. There are Godzilla-sized galaxies that resemble giant eggs, and smaller, shapeless dwarf galaxies that look like blobs of Jell-O that fell on the floor—*ker-splat!*

The grand Milky Way galaxy is almost as old as the universe itself. Formed in a large, spherical cloud of cold, swirling gas and dust about 13.6 billion years ago, it was one of the first galaxies to spread light in the dark universe. Galaxies are not peppered randomly across the skies. Instead, they are found in small clusters that make up local groups that travel through space together.

If we could launch ourselves into space and hover above the Milky Way looking straight down, we'd see a softly glowing, pinwheel-shaped group of stars approximately 160,000 light-years in diameter. In the center would be a galactic bulge intersected by a stellar bar measuring 10,000 light-years across. Radiating out from the center like the rays of a starfish would be four curved spiral arms. The Milky Way's inner golden glow results from countless stars embedded in its interior, surrounded by enough gas and dust to make billions more stars. The curved spiral arms were the last parts of our galaxy to form, and this is where our sun and solar system are located.

The Milky Way spins slowly like a giant Ferris wheel, completing one rotation every 230 to 250 million Earth years. The sun orbits around the center of the Milky Way, completing one rotation about every 225 million years. Since our star formed a mere 4.6 billion years ago, our solar system has circled the Milky Way a little more than twenty times.

We know our galaxy contains billions of stars, but what else is lurking within it? Located in the cores of almost all galaxies is a giant black hole, and the Milky Way is no exception. Dense clouds of gas and dust in the direction of the constellation Sagittarius the Archer shroud this black hole as it devours stars, planets, and anything else that strays too close. Since it first formed, this black hole has continued to feast and grow.

Stars, gas, and dusty nebulae remain the most visible components of the Milky Way, but there is something as yet unseen that makes up 27 percent of this galaxy. It is called dark matter. We cannot see dark matter, but scientists know it's out there because they can measure how its gravity interacts with the visible matter like stars in our galaxy. This mysterious gravitational force holds the rotating Milky Way galaxy together and keeps it from flying apart. Someday, someone is going to make history when they discover what dark matter really is. Could it be *you*?

Measuring the distances to objects in the Milky Way using miles or kilometers is like trying to measure the height of the Empire State Building in millionths of an inch. It doesn't make sense. Instead of miles or kilometers, scientists use the astronomical yardstick of light-years.

The more distant an object is in space, the longer it takes for its light to reach us here on Earth. Telescopes are really time machines that are always revealing the past (when light left a celestial object), not the present (when we see that light). Astronomers use the term "lookback time" to describe this phenomenon.

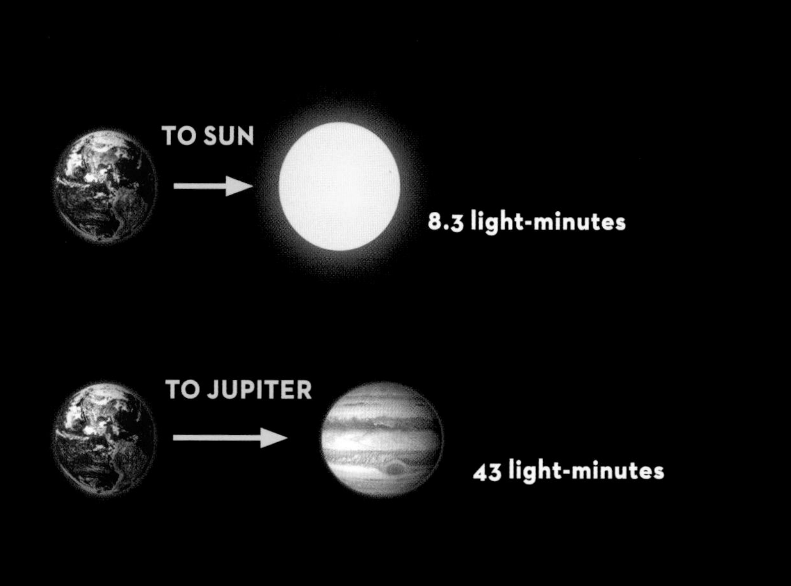
TO SUN
8.3 light-minutes
TO JUPITER
43 light-minutes

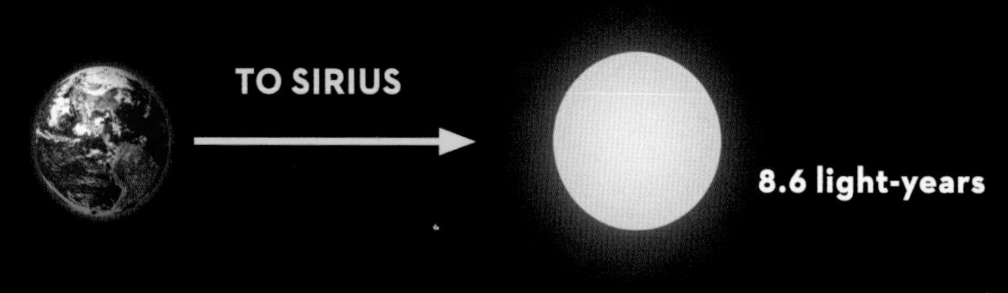
TO SIRIUS
8.6 light-years

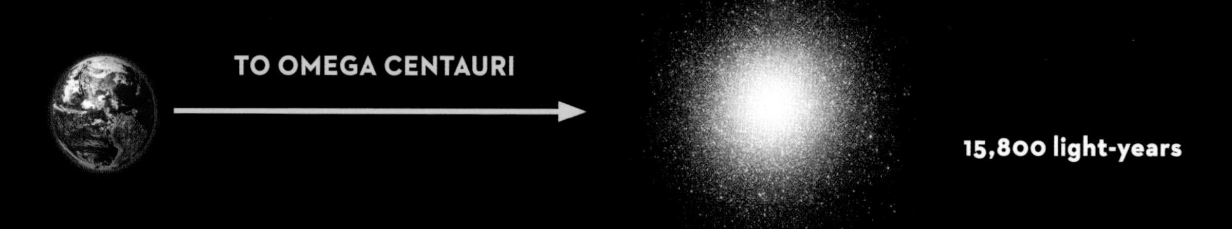
TO OMEGA CENTAURI
15,800 light-years

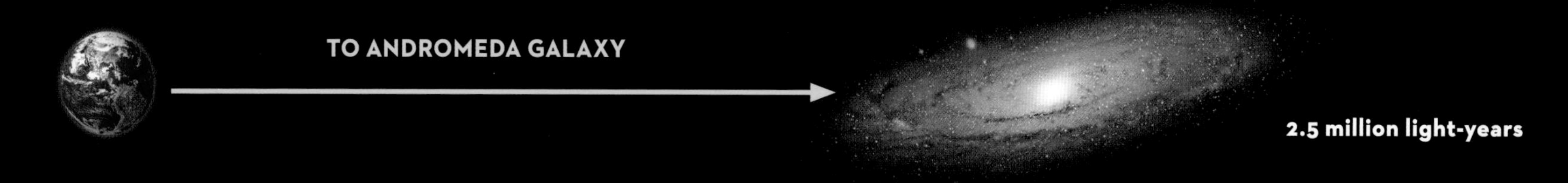
TO ANDROMEDA GALAXY
2.5 million light-years

TO MACS0647-JD
13.3 billion light-years

SIRIUS
OUR SUN

RED DWARF
(TRAPPIST-1)

Light and its energy travel through the universe like invisible ocean waves at a constant speed of 186,282 miles (299,792 km) per second. At this velocity, light waves can travel from the Earth to our moon in about 1.3 seconds. If we accelerated to the speed of light, we could fly around the Earth 7.5 times in one second, or rocket onto the surface of the sun in about eight minutes—bad move, because the solar surface is a searing 10,000° F (5,600° C) and we'd burn up—or we could jet out to the tops of the clouds on Jupiter in about forty-three minutes and freeze!

Our sun is just one of billions of stars found in our Milky Way. Astronomers know that stars vary immensely in size, color, and temperature and that more than half of them in our galaxy are older than our sun. Our sun is a midsize yellow star that formed 4.6 billion years ago and measures about 865,000 miles (1.392 million km) in diameter. You could fit 109 Earths across the face of it. Some stars, like Sirius or Vega, are more than twice the size of our sun. They shine much brighter and burn through their hydrogen fuel much more quickly than smaller stars do.

But wait a minute! Eighty percent of all stars in the Milky Way are classified as tiny red dwarfs, some less than one-eighth the size of our sun. Red dwarfs burn for trillions of years instead of billions like the sun. Since the beginning of the universe, astronomers have not detected one red dwarf star that has run out of fuel and faded away. Not only do red dwarfs appear to shine almost forever, Earthlike planets orbiting around them may be the most compelling candidates for harboring alien life in the galaxy.

From our vantage point on the surface of a small blue planet located inside one of the arms of the Milky Way galaxy, how do we confirm life is out there? The answer lies in constructing bigger and better telescopes and instruments capable of detecting fainter and more distant objects.

Since the telescope was first used to explore the heavens in the seventeenth century, optical instruments have grown in size and capability, constantly revealing more about our galaxy and the universe beyond. In 1924, astronomer Edwin Hubble, using the 100-inch telescope at Mount Wilson, announced that all those small smudges of light astronomers were seeing on photographic plates were not nearby solar systems forming but actually distant galaxies like our own Milky Way. Suddenly the universe became much larger than anyone had ever imagined.

Modern technology has opened doors to reveal new discoveries like dark matter, the mystifying force called dark energy, and the confirmation of Earthlike planets orbiting nearby stars. Now the grandest exploration of our galaxy is about to begin. Soon, four new observatories will peer into the Milky Way, probing the secrets of the heavens. The orbiting James Webb Space Telescope (JWST), developed by NASA and its international partners, will launch in 2020. The JWST carries sophisticated infrared cameras capable of

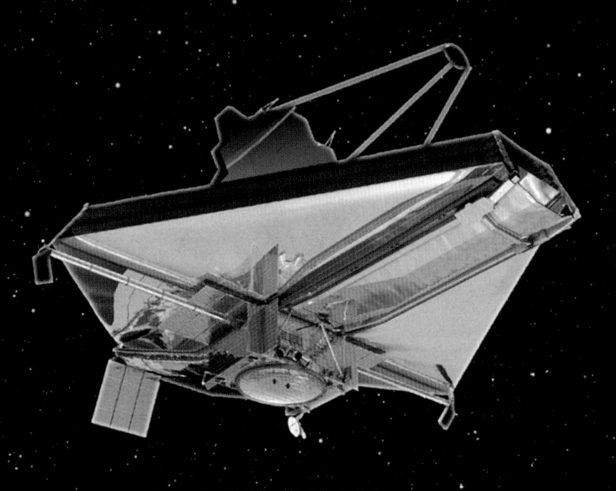

JAMES WEBB SPACE TELESCOPE

THIRTY METER TELESCOPE
Maunakea, Hawaii

penetrating through dust clouds, deep into the core of the Milky Way to reveal new solar systems in the process of forming and provide more details on the massive black holes located there. Within the next decade, three more advanced, ground-based observatories—the Giant Magellan Telescope, the Thirty Meter Telescope, and the Extremely Large Telescope—will begin systematic hunts for life in our galaxy. Analyzing the atmospheres of distant worlds may lead to the first confirmation that we are not alone. This clearly is the next giant leap in our understanding of who we are and how we Earthlings fit in with the rest of the cosmos. No doubt about it: our Milky Way galaxy will remain a fascinating and mysterious place to explore for a long time to come.

GIANT MAGELLAN TELESCOPE
Atacama Region, Chile

EXTREMELY LARGE TELESCOPE
Cerro Armazones, Chile

THE GREAT NEBULA IN ORION

STELLAR NURSERY

IF YOU LIVE in the northern hemisphere, look toward the south on a cold, clear January night and you will see three bright stars aligned in a perfect row. These stellar all-stars, Mintaka, Alnilam, and Alnitak (from left to right), form the belt of the constellation Orion the Hunter. Above and to the left of Orion's belt, the colossal orange-red star Betelgeuse (pronounced "Beetle-juice") shines brightly. Below and to the right of the belt, the sapphire-blue giant star Rigel blazes. Orion the Hunter traverses the eastern horizon in late fall, his left arm raised and wielding a club, his right arm holding a shield to protect him from his fierce opponent, Taurus the Bull. In ancient Greek mythology, Orion was the son of the sea god Poseidon, placed in the heavens after being fatally stung by a scorpion. In J. R. R. Tolkien's mythologies, he is known as Menelvagor, the "Swordsman of the Sky." In Spain and throughout Latin America, the stars of Orion's belt are called the "Three Marys." The ancient Aztecs knew these stars as the "Fire Drill." Their appearance

in the eastern sky signaled it was time for the New Fire ceremony, a ritual performed long ago to ensure our fragile world would survive another year and not suddenly end. Luckily for us, it appears to have worked!

Below Orion's belt, you will find a curved line of stars that extends down, forming his sword. Look toward the center of that line and you'll notice a faint hazy glow, easily seen with the unaided eye. (It will stand out even more if you use a pair of binoculars.) What is this glowing patch of light? Astronomers know it as M42, the Great Nebula in Orion. For us, it is numero uno of the seven wonders of the Milky Way!

The Great Nebula in Orion is a massive cloud of gas and dust that is nearly 25 light-years in diameter. If we could travel there at the speed of light (and who wouldn't want to?), our journey would last 1,300 years. This means the light you see coming from the Great Nebula in Orion left there 1,300 years ago, or about the year 718, just before the first water-powered mechanical clock was invented in China.

It would take another twenty-five years to fly from one edge of the Great Nebula to the other. But our trip would be rewarded, for this nebula—composed of lofty pillars of colorful gas and dust—is something quite special. Buried deep inside its interstellar tapestry are thousands of new fledgling stars that have just been born. Say hello, baby stars! The Great Nebula is the nearest and largest stellar nursery in our sky. It also provides the perfect laboratory to study how new stars and new solar systems form.

In the center of the Great Nebula shine four luminous and very massive stars known as the Trapezium. They are named for the trapezoid, a four-sided geometric shape with a pair of opposite sides that aren't parallel. Ultraviolet light and fierce solar winds unleashed by these giant blue-white Trapezium stars have carved a hole in the middle of the nebula, slowing down or stopping the formation of hundreds of other, smaller stars.

As new stars come together out of swirling gas clouds, older and bigger stars can bring the process to a halt. Their stronger solar winds blast star-forming material back into space, just like blowing on a dandelion.

Peering deep into these same nebular clouds, we also see tiny brown dwarf stars nested in the Great Nebula. Brown dwarf stars do not have enough stellar material to form nuclear-powered stars like our sun. They are static objects caught in the middle of stellar formation. Brown dwarfs are too large to be considered planets like Jupiter and Saturn, and too small to shine like stars.

The surreal colors revealed in images of the Great Nebula are attributed to the wide range of different mixtures of gases it contains. Red clouds are mostly hydrogen gas, the most common element in the universe. Blue and green hues contain nitrogen and oxygen, yellow gas clouds contain sodium, and dark brown clouds contain carbon and silicon dust. And there it is: a stellar paint box of critical elements. All of these atoms will become the building blocks for new stars, new planets, and any life-forms that may emerge on future worlds orbiting new suns.

In 1992 the remarkable Hubble Space Telescope uncovered something deep inside the Great Nebula that no one had ever seen before. Suspended in its billowing clouds are teardrop-shaped blobs of gas with long, comet-like tails extending millions of miles behind them. They almost look like tiny cosmic pollywogs swimming through space! Inside these ghostly shapes are new stars whose nuclear fires are just turning on. Surrounding these new protostars—or proplyds, as astronomers call them—are huge rings of gas and dust. From the material contained inside these primordial disks, new planets are forming. For the very first time, we are witnessing the genesis of solar systems, happening in the same way our own planetary neighborhood came about approximately 4.6 billion years ago.

Star formation is a process that begins in dark clouds of extremely cold gas and dust, where small, dense clumps of material bind together, contract under immense pressure, and slowly start spinning. Gravity draws the gas and dust into hotter concentrations, toward a common center where nuclear fusion results in the formation of a spectacular new star. The outer leftover material becomes planets. The biggest stars produce strong solar winds and intense radiation, which blast away the remaining surrounding cloud. During this process, new stars light up the nebula, making it visible to us. In time this life-giving nebula will vanish, leaving behind bright, open clusters of new young stars. Eventually these stellar "newborns" will drift away, just like older siblings leaving home. Our sun, now alone in outer space, went through this same process after emerging from an ancient gas cloud, one that was perhaps as remarkable as the Great Nebula. Since that time, all other stars born out of this venerable gas cloud have dispersed to new locations in our Milky Way galaxy.

Using NASA's Spitzer Space Telescope, astronomers have uncovered nearly 2,300 new stars forming deep inside the Great Nebula. Each star has a flattened disk of gas and dust that is in the process of forming new planets and solar systems. Let's stop and think about this for a minute. All around us in

space, thousands of new stars and planets are now forming, displaying the vast and beautiful cycle of life in the universe!

Everything in the universe has a beginning, middle, and end. The original nebula that gave birth to our solar system has now disappeared, and the same fate awaits the Great Nebula in Orion. Ultimately it will fade away, too. But don't be sad! This process is repeated over and over again in our Milky Way galaxy and throughout the universe. Will future spectacular star nurseries appear in our skies after the Great Nebula in Orion is gone? Fantastically, the answer is yes! Astronomers recently discovered what may be the next Orion-type star-forming nebula, in the regal constellation Cassiopeia. Shaped like a big W in the northern sky, Queen Cassiopeia is positioned opposite the Big Dipper. This new nebula, called W3, has just begun to shine, reflecting the light generated by newborn stars inside it. Shrouds of dark dust currently hide most of the light radiated by these new stars, but this darkened state is temporary. In a hundred thousand years—a long time for Earthlings but only a blink of the eye for the universe—W3 will blaze forth, delighting stargazers throughout our part of the Milky Way galaxy. This nebula is destined to emerge as the new Great Nebula in Cassiopeia and become visible to Earthlings living anywhere in our solar system or beyond. It's fun to think that someday a new wonder may replace a current wonder in our Milky Way galaxy!

OMEGA CENTAURI

OLDEST STARS IN THE MILKY WAY

OUR UNIVERSE SPARKED into life 13.8 billion years ago with a cosmic event known as the Big Bang. The simplest atoms in the cosmos—hydrogen and helium—were the first predominant elements to form after this brief but monumental episode in time. Today astronomers know that hydrogen atoms make up 90 percent of all elements in the universe. Hydrogen, with one positive-charged proton in the nucleus and one negative-charged electron encircling it, is the smallest, lightest, and least complicated atom ever known. At the beginning of the universe, hydrogen, along with helium, deuterium, and lithium atoms, produced the first stars that illuminated the dark heavens. As more stars emerged from mammoth nebular gas clouds like the Great Nebula in Orion, they congregated into larger masses called galaxies. Our fantastic Milky Way came into existence during this time period. However, galaxies were not the first structures in this new universe to form. Something else preceded them: globular clusters. These spherical globes of densely packed stars were the first to emerge around the centers of shapeless primordial galaxies. Looking like giant swarms of cosmic bees, globular clusters shine with some of the oldest stars in the universe. The ancient Greeks revered the only globular cluster visible to the naked eye as one of the most luminous of all the objects in the sky. Today we know it as Omega Centauri. Truly in a class all by itself, it shall be crowned "Wonder #2" in our galactic journey through the stars.

Nearly all galaxies are surrounded by swarms of globular clusters. We can observe at least 450 of them in our nearest and brightest neighbor, the Andromeda galaxy. Our local Milky Way doesn't have quite as many. Early on, our globular cluster count may have scored higher, but over time, many collided in spectacular stellar smash-ups, reducing the count to no more than 150 monster hives. Globular clusters are found orbiting the outskirts of galaxies in an area called the galactic halo. This may sound heavenly, but these spherical halos hold an enormous reservoir of hot gas and recycled star material. Many of the ancient stars in these clusters are more than eleven billion years old, more than twice the age of our sun. That's really ancient!

In the northern hemisphere, amateur astronomers can view the globular cluster M13 in the constellation Hercules. Not quite visible to the naked eye, it is easily picked out with a pair of binoculars on a moonless night, appearing as a fuzzy star. In the southern hemisphere, something much grander awaits. Located 15,800 light-years from Earth, the king of globular clusters, Omega Centauri, is found in the constellation Centaurus the Centaur. The light seen tonight from Omega Centauri left there 15,800 years ago, when Stone Age artists were painting colorful renderings of animals and human hunters on the walls of caves in what is now southern France.

Blazing against the rich, dense star clouds of the Milky Way, Omega Centauri is the largest globular cluster in our galaxy. Measuring roughly 150 light-years in diameter, it encompasses at least ten million stars. It also may have once been the central core of an "I'm-just-passing-by" dwarf galaxy that was captured by the Milky Way. Located low on the horizon, Omega Centauri can be seen from southern states like Arizona, Texas, and especially Florida during the spring and early summer months. But the southern hemisphere,

Omega Centauri, the largest and brightest globular cluster in the Milky Way, looks like a swarm of buzzing bees.

in places like Chile or Australia, claims the best view of all, where it is easily spotted with the naked eye. Of all the globular clusters known to science, Omega Centauri is the finest and most awe-inspiring.

Many astronomers wonder if there might be life-forms more advanced than we are inside these star clusters. After all, these stars have existed more than twice as long as our sun and our solar system. Is Omega Centauri where we should be looking for radio broadcasts or laser bursts that signal a distant star civilization? First, we have to consider this: Measuring the content of stars located inside globular clusters, we find they contain twenty times less heavy metals than stars like our sun. (We think of metals as being hard shiny materials like gold or silver that are mined from the ground. Astronomers use the term "metal" to describe any elements found in stars other than hydrogen and helium gas.) But this doesn't mean stars in Omega Centauri are lightweights! It only means that since they lack these heavier elements, life as we know it may not exist inside globular clusters. There's a good chance that planets like Earth, with molten iron cores, might not be found there either. Do you know why life needs heavy elements like iron to exist? The answer is found in sweet biology.

All living things on Earth use metals in their bodies to function. Plants need phosphates and potassium to grow. Metals help us maintain healthy immune systems. They assist the body in repairing itself, and they make insulin to help convert sugars into energy. Metals in our bloodstreams can also act like microscopic moving vans or transport carriers. What color is your blood when you skin your knee or cut your finger? It's red! The heavy element iron colors your blood cells red. It is not there just for looks; it attaches oxygen molecules to our blood cells, distributing energy from our lungs through our bloodstream to our muscles, organs, and brain. Crustaceans like crabs and lobsters have greenish-colored copper in their bloodstream to do the same thing. Insects use the yellow-colored metal sodium to distribute oxygen to cells in their bodies. All these heavier elements were forged in the cores of supernova explosions billions of years after the first stars in globular clusters formed. This sounds bizarre, I know. Without heavy metals dispersed on planetary surfaces inside globular clusters, life as we know it might not exist. These would be worlds without iron, copper, silicon, manganese, nickel, sodium, aluminum, silver, or gold to kick-start primary life-forms or later to help build things like cars, buildings, mountain bikes, airplanes, video games, computers, or telescopes to search for life in the rest of the universe. Whew!

Recently, using the Hubble Space Telescope, astronomers have identified many younger, second-generation stars inside globular clusters that appear

Planets orbiting stars closely bound together inside globular clusters like Omega Centauri may undergo constant bombardment from comets and asteroids crashing down on their surfaces.

Any life existing deep within Omega Centauri would see a night sky ablaze with light. With so many stars filling their view, it might be impossible to glimpse anything beyond their ancient cluster of stars.

to have higher metal content than that of their ancient relatives. With a higher metal content, these newer stars may host solar systems capable of supporting life, but any living organisms within these clusters may be threatened by their own environment. Stars in globular clusters are jam-packed together, separated by less than one-tenth of a light-year. With stars crammed so close, nearby stars can disrupt each other's orbits, possibly stripping off orbiting planets and flinging them into space. There could be spectacular cosmic collisions happening as well. Tossed about by these changing gravitational influences, and with asteroids and comets raining down on their surfaces, these worlds may exist in cosmic chaos!

In very dark night skies far from brilliant city lights, we might see upward of three thousand to four thousand stars. Standing on a planet located deep inside Omega Centauri, we'd find the sky ablaze with glowing stars. This epic blast of light radiating from tens of thousands of stars is bright enough to cast shadows along the ground on this alien world. To someone on that planet gazing out, even the darkest night would exhibit an odd twilight glow, lit by a grainy tapestry of countless stars. Overhead, a mix of brilliant blue stars, orange-colored red giant stars, white stars, and red dwarfs would present a bejeweled sky twenty times brighter than our night sky during a full moon. Could alien astronomers see beyond Omega Centauri? It's possible they might detect a distant galaxy through this zoo of overhead stars, but with such a luminous sky, the chances are slim. Lacking radio or ultraviolet telescopes to pierce the skies, they might not know of anything else beyond their own fierce ball of stars. In their supreme stellar isolation, Omega Centauri would seem to comprise everything that existed in their universe.

When stars reach old age, they puff up in size and become cooler in temperature in what astronomers call their red giant phase. UY Scuti is the largest red giant star known in the universe. It has a diameter more than 1,700 times larger than our sun.

UY SCUTI

BIGGEST STAR IN THE MILKY WAY

SO FAR IN our grand road trip through the Milky Way, we've encountered some real cosmic characters! We've seen new stars emerging inside a gigantic stellar nursery and encountered primordial stars clinging to the fringes of our galaxy. We've learned that without stars, the universe would be engulfed in darkness. Shining stars send light, heat, and energetic solar winds through space. When we watch our own star set, the fading daylight is soon replaced by a sky full of twinkly gems whose light has traveled across unimaginable distances in space. Each blazing point of light represents a potentially life-sustaining star. Stars are such incredible powerhouses, it's no wonder our society calls someone a "star" when they've done something particularly well.

Did you know that our sun is a medium-size star? Many of the stars seen in the night sky are much larger. It's a fact. Our sun is classified as a yellow G star, measuring not quite one million miles in diameter. Now let's compare our sun to the dazzling bluish-white star Vega, located in the constellation Lyra the Harp. More than twice the diameter of our sun, Vega blazes overhead in the northern hemisphere during summertime and is affectionately known as the "Sapphire Star of Summer." This speedy giant spins so fast it's not round. Instead, Vega is shaped more like an Easter egg. If we jump forward in time to winter, the colossal orange-red star Betelgeuse radiates from the constellation Orion the Hunter. It is a monstrous dying star, easily a thousand times larger than our sun, or roughly a billion miles in diameter. Can you imagine seeing this red supergiant up close? For the longest time, astronomers thought Betelgeuse was the biggest star in the galaxy. But pardon me: *buzz* . . . wrong answer! This esteemed honor belongs to a star found in the constellation Scutum, which means "the shield." May I present UY Scuti, a star of such stellar proportions that it has become our third wonder of the Milky Way galaxy!

Early in the last century, astronomers discovered that not all stars were alike in size, age, or temperature. An astronomy assistant named Annie Jump Cannon made this remarkable discovery in 1901 while working at the Harvard College Observatory in Cambridge, Massachusetts. Her official job title was "computer"—this is true—and she was paid a whopping twenty-five cents an hour. Her task was to examine glass photographic plates and separate stars into different groups. Cannon was so good at this, she could analyze and classify up to three stars a minute. Ultimately, Cannon identified seven different groups of stars based on their sizes and temperatures. It's significant that the original star classification system she created is still in use today: OBAFGKM. What do Cannon's letters mean? O stars are the biggest and hottest of all stars. They are blue and, due to their higher core temperatures, burn through their hydrogen fuel in just a few million years. They are the gas-guzzlers of the universe! B, A, and F stars are hot blue-white stars that shine for two to six billion years. G stars, like our sun, are yellow and exist for about ten billion years.

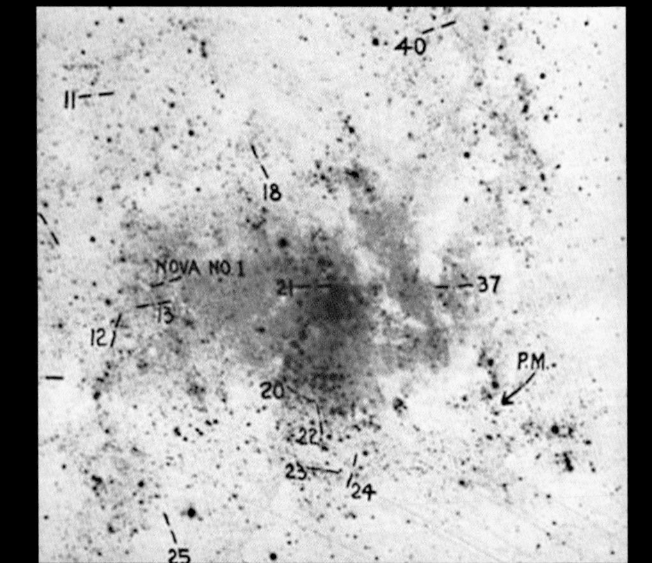

ABOVE: Annie Jump Cannon, 1930s.

RIGHT: An example of one of the photographic plates that led to Cannon's stellar discoveries.

The smaller K stars are orange, and they can shine for twelve to fourteen billion years. The smallest and coolest, M stars are red and burn for trillions of years. All of these stars are called main-sequence stars because they are still fusing hydrogen atoms into helium atoms in their cores. About 90 percent of all the stars in the Milky Way are main-sequence stars, meaning that they are now shining through the most stable part of their lifetimes. Eventually, all main-sequence stars burn through their hydrogen fuel supply and reach the end of their life cycle. When this happens a star leaves the main sequence. *Adios, mi amigo!* As the stars' inner fires cool down, their outer layers start collapsing inward and visibly begin to shrink, until core temperatures become hot enough to fuse helium atoms into carbon atoms. News flash: This is where all the carbon atoms we find on Earth came from. They originated in the cores of ancient stars that exploded or faded away billions of years ago. Fusing helium into carbon causes the star to suddenly balloon outward, creating a red giant star several times larger than the original. This is the star's final act before it disappears forever. UY Scuti is approaching the last stages of its life. It is such an enormous red giant star that astronomers recognize it as a red hypergiant or the largest star ever detected in the universe—for now, anyway!

Astronomers use the mnemonic "Oh Be A Fine Girl (Guy) Kiss Me" to remember Annie Jump Cannon's classification list of stars. She began with an earlier list of twenty-two alphabetical classifications, and then rearranged and condensed it down to seven letters. Each letter identifies how hot a type of star is; O stars are the hottest, and M stars the coolest.

Red giant stars approaching the end of their lives tend to be cooler than smaller stars and do not send out light in wavelengths our eyes can see. Some can appear dim in the sky to us, but UY Scuti shines loudly and proudly as one of the most luminous stars in the galaxy. At a distance of 9,500 light-years, this means the light we see tonight from UY Scuti left there 9,500 years ago, when humans were still hunter-gatherers and had begun domesticating sheep and making pottery. UY Scuti is also a variable star, meaning it expands and contracts and expands again in size. It does this every 740 days, alternately shrinking and expanding like an extremely slow-beating heart!

Comparing the size of UY Scuti to that of other stars definitely challenges our brains. The size of this star is tough to visualize, but let's give it a try. Earth is close to 8,000 miles (12,875 km) in diameter. Now imagine that the Earth was reduced down to the size of a professional soccer ball, having a diameter of 9 inches (23 cm). Using the same ratio, our sun would be about 75 feet (23 m) in diameter, or as tall as a seven-story building! Our favorite queen, the blue-white star Vega that reigns overhead during summer in the northern hemisphere, would clock in at 210 feet (64 m) in diameter, or the height of a twenty-one-story skyscraper! Can we go bigger?

Yes, we can. Blazing Arcturus, a star visible in spring and summertime, would measure 1,875 feet (572 m) in diameter. That's about six stories higher than One World Trade Center in New York. Is your brain keeping up with these enormous sizes? Just how much larger could we go by applying our scale to supersized UY Scuti? At 25 miles (40 km) in diameter, Scuti would win. If UY Scuti replaced the sun in our solar system, it would extend far out beyond the orbit of Jupiter.

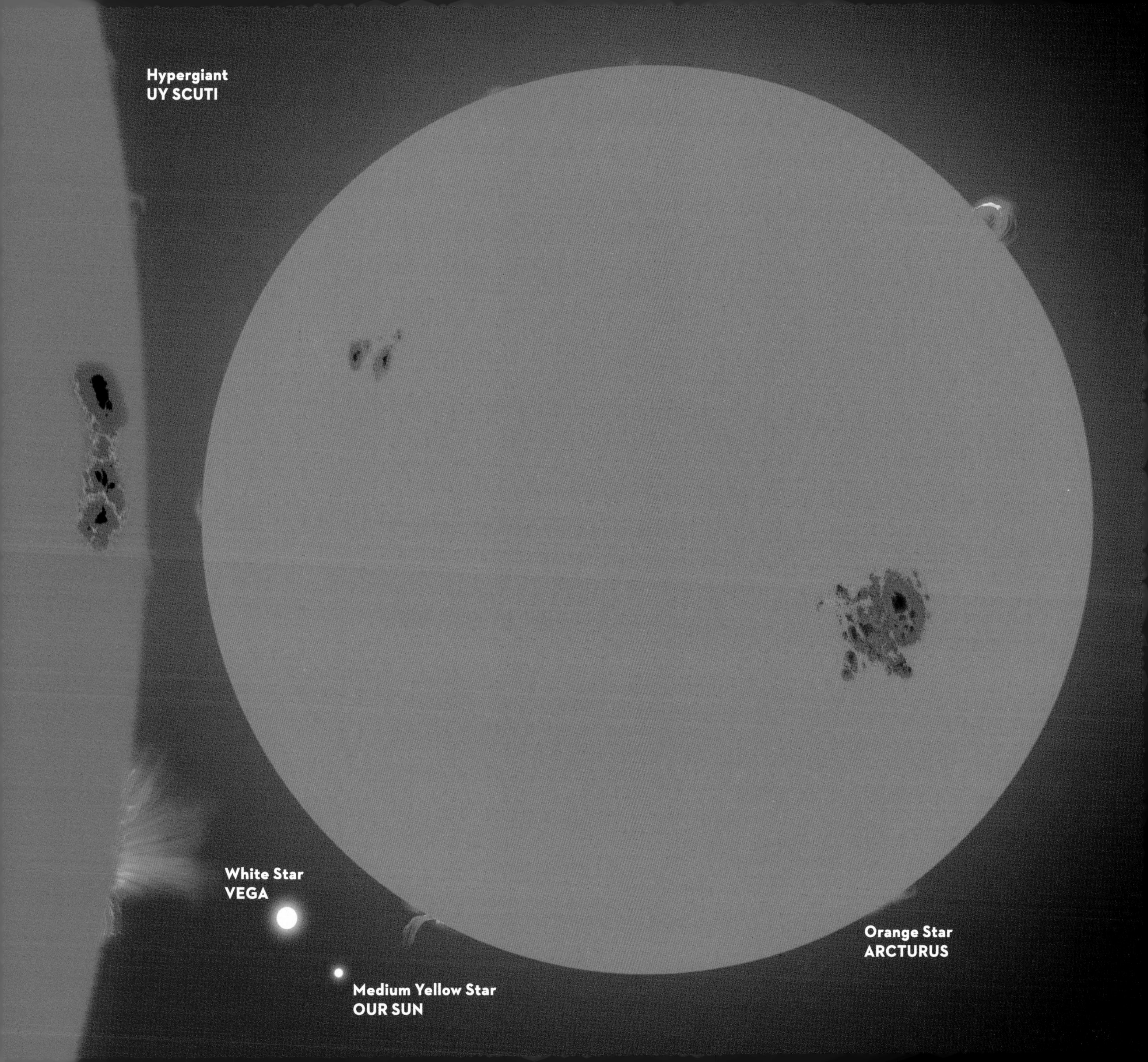

Hypergiant
UY SCUTI

White Star
VEGA

Orange Star
ARCTURUS

Medium Yellow Star
OUR SUN

Major stars like UY Scuti do not go quietly into the night! When they finally exhaust all their atomic fuel, disaster strikes. As the nuclear fires in their cores begin to cool, gravity becomes the dominant force, and the stars begin to collapse like balloons losing their air. Once this collapse begins, it is unstoppable. Pressure builds, heating the core and creating soaring temperatures. The final result is that the star either explodes violently or continues collapsing and disappears into oblivion, transforming itself into an awesome black hole.

The best scientific models for UY Scuti predict it will remain a red hypergiant for a few million years before its fatal collapse begins, resulting in a massive supernova. Since UY Scuti is located relatively close to Earth, it is possible that humans could witness this star's final spectacular moments as it lights up the nighttime sky. It may even be visible in the daytime sky for months. When this happens, the largest star identified in our universe will have self-detonated, sending out massive amounts of energy and clouds of gas and dust that will someday be reincorporated into new stars and solar systems. The perpetual solar cycle will begin again. What a wonderful lesson about how matter in the Milky Way is recycled. We truly do live in a "green" universe.

J1407B

STRANGEST PLANET IN THE MILKY WAY

SINCE THE FIRST confirmed exoplanet was discovered in 1992, astronomers now realize the universe is overflowing with new worlds. Exoplanets are planets located outside our solar system. The prefix *exo-* is from the Greek language, meaning "outside." (Ever accidentally step on a bug? If you did, you would see there are no bones hidden inside its body. Its hard outer shell forms an exoskeleton, or a skeleton on the "outside" of the insect.) In the growing field of exoplanet research, it's estimated that our Milky Way galaxy harbors more than a hundred billion different alien worlds. This seems unimaginable, but research shows that many resemble those commonly found in our solar system: small, rocky terrestrial worlds, gas and ice giants, and a host of dwarf planets.

Next are the super-weird planets like CoRoT-7b. Here it rains rocks. This "exo" is nearly twice the size of Earth. It also orbits dangerously close to its star, almost twenty-three times closer than Mercury orbits our sun. CoRoT-7b is a real hothead, too! With surface temperatures soaring to 4,000° F (2,200° C), surface rock gets zapped (vaporized), evaporates into the air, and then cools down just enough to solidify back into pebbles. But the show isn't over yet. These rocks then rain back down, pelting the living daylights out of CoRoT-7b's surface.

Then there's the first exoplanet to have its picture taken, planet 55 Cancri e. It's located approximately 40 light-years away and is about twice the size of Earth, making it what scientists call a super-Earth. "Super-duper Earth" is more like it, because 55 Cancri e is—wait for it—worth 30 nonillion dollars. If you want to write this out, it's $30 followed by thirty zeros. That's some serious alien cash! Unlike Earth, this rocky planet does not have oceans or granite rocks covering its surface. Instead, it is blanketed by black graphite derived from carbon, the same material used in pencils but here compressed down through heat and pressure into pure diamonds. So we can say, "Shine on, 55 Cancri e!"

Finally, we must consider the exoplanet WASP-1b, a gas giant planet that orbits its star in just one day and absorbs 94 percent of the light shining on its surface. Blacker than a lump of asphalt, WASP-1b is the darkest planet ever discovered.

These bizarre and unexpected worlds spark our imagination and make us wonder: What else may be hidden in the depths of space?

Ready? Here goes! Located 433 light-years away from Earth, in the constellation Centaurus, is a star that appears to be blinking. The star is not turning on and off; it is being covered, then uncovered, then covered up again by a very strange eclipsing planet. Astronomers have never witnessed this type of fluctuation before. Named J1407b, this massive exoplanet is many, many times larger than Jupiter. And move over, Saturn: This planet's ring system makes yours look like chump change. Astronomers nicknamed J1407b "Monster Saturn with Super-Rings," and we now hail it as our fourth wonder of the Milky Way galaxy.

In our solar system, we find many planets with rings. Saturn's magnificent ring system resembles a majestic golden crown. Jupiter's rings, as well as those of Uranus and Neptune, are not quite as impressive. In fact, astronomers didn't spot Jupiter's rings until the *Voyager* spacecraft flew close by and looked back toward the Earth. The rings emerged when they were illuminated by light from our own distant sun. This was a very exciting discovery!

You may not know that long ago the Earth had rings, too. During the early formation of our solar system 4.5 billion years ago, a planetary object about the size of Mars crashed into Earth, blasting rocks and debris into orbit around our planet. Held tightly by Earth's gravity, the debris first spread out, forming a beautiful ring system around our world. Over the next few million years, heat generated

Backlit by the distant sun emerging above its upper edge, Jupiter's rings suddenly became visible to the passing *Voyager 1* spacecraft in 1979.

through relentless impacts fused these debris particles together, forging a new companion to Earth that we now call the moon.

With five of our planets sporting rings at one time or another in their history, we might suppose that planets with rings are common elsewhere in space. Today, astronomers have found the answer, and it is stunning. The distant exoplanet J1407b has a ring system that extends 75 million miles (120 million km) in diameter, or two hundred times larger across than the rings of Saturn! With its ring system consisting of about thirty-seven separate ringlets, we're inclined to call J1407b the all-new Lord of the Rings!

Most exoplanets are so far away, they are too small to be seen with telescopes, but we can detect them when they pass in front of a star. When this occurs, the exoplanet blocks out some of the stellar light, causing the star to dim a bit. It is easy for astronomers to observe and record this tiny dip in starlight. Typically, when a big, Jupiter-sized planet crosses in front of a star, it blocks about 1 percent of the light. Think of it like this: 1 percent is comparable to the amount of light a mosquito would block if it flew in front of a car's headlight. When the main star J1407a appeared to blink on and off, observers were actually witnessing J1407b's gargantuan rings passing across the face of the star, blocking out almost 95 percent of the star's light. With this significant reduction in starlight, researchers realized the ring system had to be massive. If we put the planet J1407b in place of our

sun, its rings would stretch out seven million miles beyond the orbit of Venus!

Even more enticing, there are gaps in the rings, indicating new moons are forming in the open spaces. This follows the same formation process experienced by Jupiter's four moons—Io, Europa, Ganymede, and Callisto—some 4.5 billion years ago. They too condensed out of a gigantic flat ring of gas and dust, this one orbiting Jupiter. Can you visualize this? For the first time, we are witnessing the birth of new alien moons around a distant world. Of particular interest to astronomers studying J1407b is a recently discovered large gap in the rings. This area is so wide, it appears a satellite moon has already formed. This new moon is probably the size of Earth or Mars, and a planetary body this large should be able to retain an atmosphere. If we compare J1407b's humongous orbit to the orbits of the planets in our solar system, this lunar object would be located somewhere between the orbits of Mars and Jupiter. There might not be any life

on the giant planet itself, but what are the odds that life might someday exist on a planet-sized moon? Heat generated by the gravitational attraction between the main planet, J1407b, and its moon could make this satellite quite warm and balmy, creating optimum conditions for life to exist. Billions of years from now, this may be an ideal location for biologists from Earth to visit. Here they may uncover a budding paradise with emerging life blanketing it.

One of the greatest mysteries of this monstrous ring system is why it still exists. Even though J1407b and its sun are only sixteen million years old, the gravitational effects of the planet's non-circular orbit should have ripped the rings apart long ago. Ah, a mystery like this is something scientists really like to work on. A little space sleuthing is in order then. The answer might have something to do with the spin of the rings. Planet J1407b does not orbit its star in a circle. It orbits in an oval-shaped path instead. When the massive spinning rings come closest to their star, they are at the greatest risk of breaking up. If the rings were rotating clockwise (to the right, like the hands on a clock), they would be toast; the rings would have spiraled into the star and been shredded long ago! However, if they rotate counterclockwise (to the left, or opposite the direction the hands on a clock move), they would survive. In a few more million years, all the dust in these rings will be used up in forming new moons. The rings will gradually become more ghostlike, until they vanish completely into the cosmos.

It can be difficult to visualize how spectacular some of these wonders in faraway star systems really are. To us, they appear as tiny dots on charts and graphs. So we look to our own imagination and apply good science to understand and appreciate these unseen treasures. If somehow we could magically replace Saturn's rings with those of J1407b, the resulting sight would be dazzling! This spectacle of rings would be easily visible during day or night and would appear many times larger than a rising harvest moon. In fact, the rings would reflect so much sunlight, they would outshine a full moon!

TRAPPIST-1

MOST EARTHLIKE PLANETS IN THE MILKY WAY

UNTIL A FEW years ago, scientists maintained that all solar systems throughout the universe might be similar to ours. Smaller, warmer terrestrial planets would be found orbiting close to their stars, and gas and ice giants would be found cruising farther away in the much colder solar suburbs, while tiny dwarf planets populated the farthest icy outback regions. This was a fair assumption—however, it was wrong.

Astronomers had a big surprise when the first exoplanets discovered were Jupiter-sized worlds orbiting so close to their stars, each orbit was completed in hours or days instead of years. Because they were so near their stars, these exoplanets were searingly hot. Astronomers quickly dubbed them "hot Jupiters," and what followed was a bonanza of new planet discoveries.

Early in the twenty-first century, planets smaller than Jupiter and Saturn started being detected on a regular basis by NASA's Kepler space telescope, and the quest was on to identify other Earthlike planets. To be considered Earthlike, these newfound alien worlds had to meet special criteria: They had to be about the size of Earth, orbit a star similar to our sun, and be located at a desirable distance from their

host star. Why would distance be so important? Life as we know it needs water to survive. So if we want to identify other worlds where life like ours might exist, the planet-star orbital distance needs to be just right. Too close? All your oceans and atmosphere boil away. Too far away? Everything freezes. If a planet is located at the correct orbital distance from its star, where water can exist as a liquid, as a solid like ice, and as a vapor, it is considered to be in the "habitable zone."

Discovering one Earthlike planet orbiting in the habitable zone around a distant star is unique. Identifying two would be close to a miracle. Finding three sounds like science fiction! Welcome to the fifth wonder of the Milky Way galaxy, TRAPPIST-1. This is a star with seven Earth-size planets orbiting around it, and three of them are in the magic habitable zone.

Our Milky Way is host to between two hundred and four hundred billion stars. The search for planets that may support life focuses on the habitable zones around sun-like stars and red dwarf stars (like TRAPPIST-1), one of the most abundant types of stars in the universe.

Most red dwarf stars emit energy in wavelengths our eyes cannot see. They radiate mostly infrared light, not the colors of the rainbow to which our eyes are sensitive. Instead, we can feel these infrared energy waves as heat. Did you know that snakes possess infrared sensors on the tips of their tongues? They use them to zero in on the infrared body heat emitted by warm-bodied mammals at night. It's another tool to help them "see" in the dark. Put a snake on a planet orbiting a red dwarf star and everything might look like potential prey!

Planets orbiting red dwarf stars are located so close to their star that one side of the planet always faces its sun, and the other side always faces away into space. We call this perpetual state "tidal locking." (Our moon is tidally locked to Earth. That's why we see only one lunar side. Did you know only orbiting spacecraft and the Apollo astronauts have seen the far side of the moon?) Planets tidally locked around red dwarf stars have no sunsets, sunrises, or seasons or changes in night and day. One side is always bathed in daylight, making it extremely warm. A so-called transition zone, or twilight zone, runs north to south around the edge of the sunlit area, like a wide stripe around a basketball; it's always in twilight. Time now to take a closer look at the TRAPPIST-1 planetary group.

For clarity, astronomers always attach the letter "a" to the name of a star. Its planets start with the letter "b" and go through the alphabet as they are discovered. The exoplanet TRAPPIST-1b orbits its star in just one and a half days. Slower TRAPPIST-1c takes two and a half days to complete one orbit, while poky -d circles around in four days. All three are

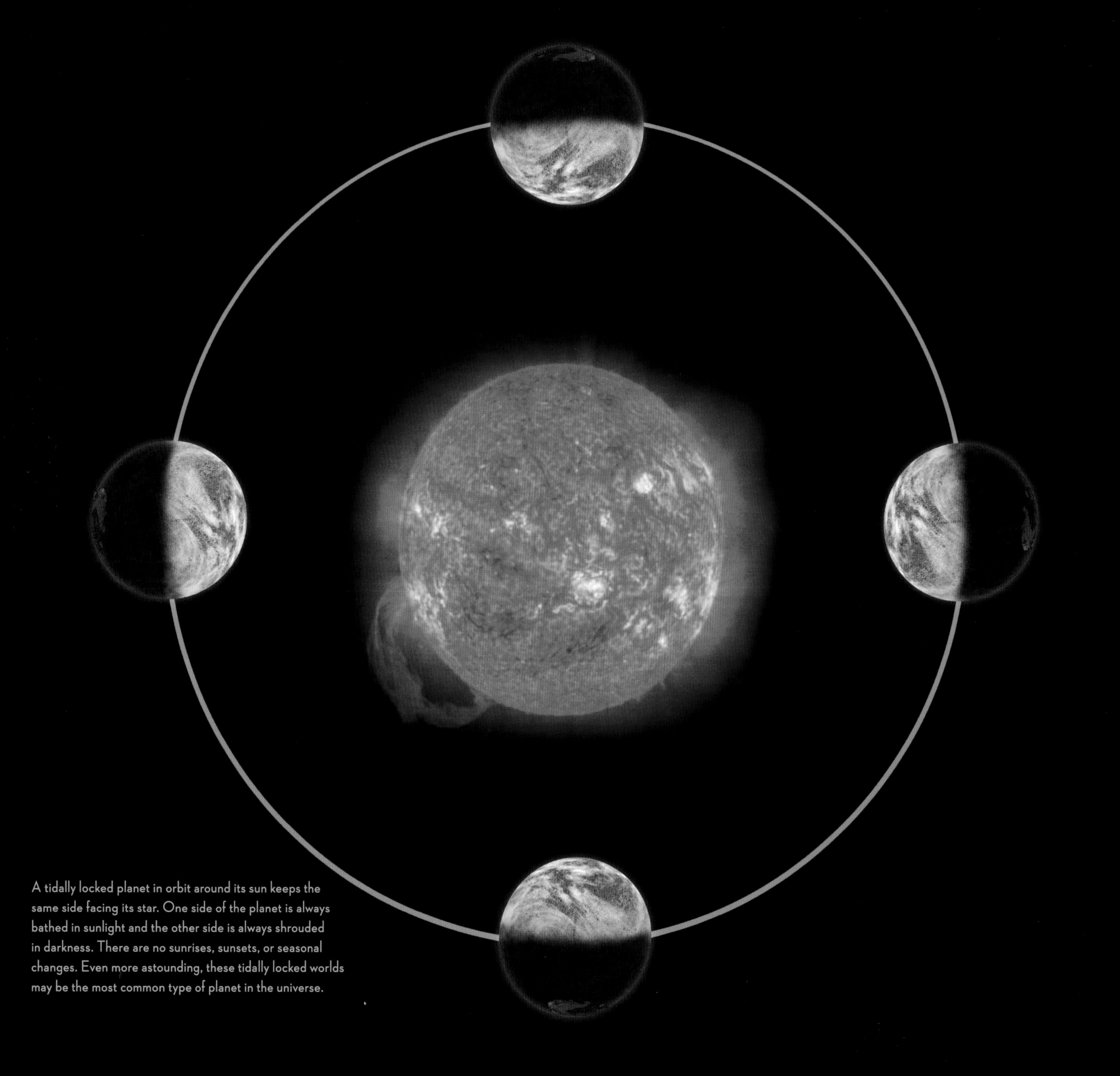

A tidally locked planet in orbit around its sun keeps the same side facing its star. One side of the planet is always bathed in sunlight and the other side is always shrouded in darkness. There are no sunrises, sunsets, or seasonal changes. Even more astounding, these tidally locked worlds may be the most common type of planet in the universe.

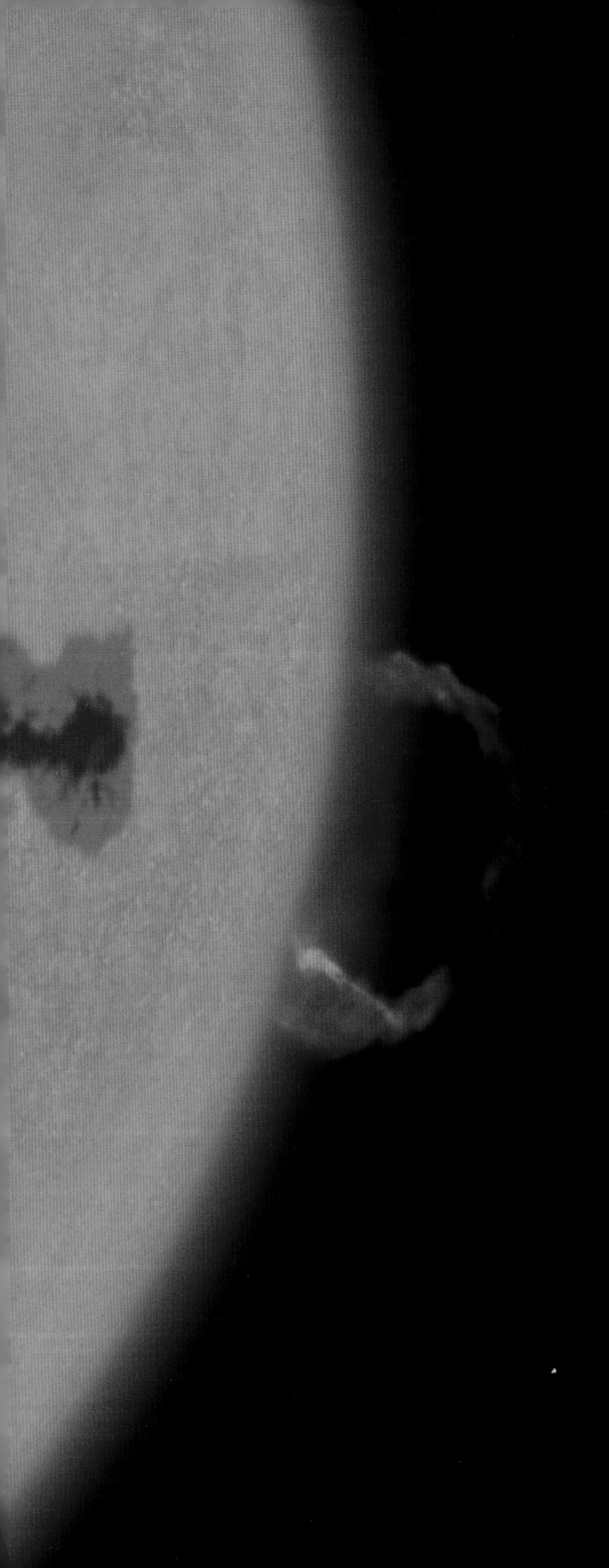

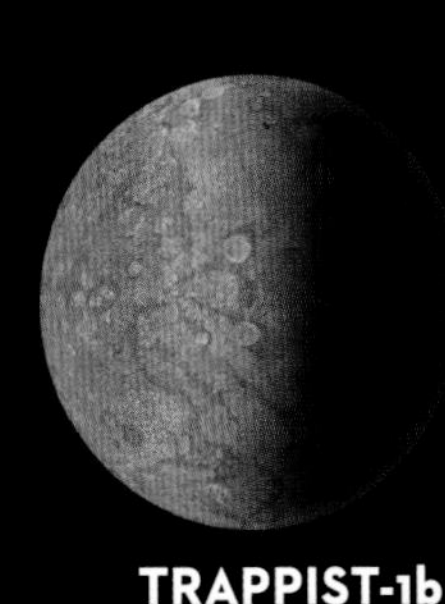

TRAPPIST-1b

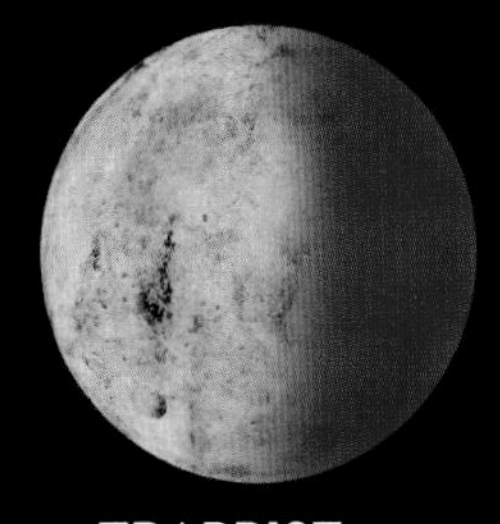

TRAPPIST-1c

TRAPPIST-1d

considered too close to their star and too hot to support life as we know it, with temperatures closer to those found on Mercury and Venus than Earth. Way-out TRAPPIST-1h, the farthest orbiting world in this system, is a planet on the edge. Located on the farthest fringes for life to exist, it is likely too cold to support liquid oceans. So we look to the remaining three planets, TRAPPIST-1e, -f, and -g—separated from each other by just a few days of spaceflight—as potential worlds that have all the essential conditions for life. But don't be fooled: TRAPPIST-1 planets are not the type of environments humans would find comfortable. Even if their atmospheres have oxygen, nitrogen, and other types of gases found here on Earth, their red dwarf star sends out tremendous amounts of radiation that for us would be equivalent to receiving a full-body X-ray every few days. Ultimately, humans could not withstand the extreme radiation hitting the surfaces of these worlds without wearing heavy, lead-lined protective space suits. Not fun!

Tidally locked worlds also display peculiar weather patterns that are not experienced here on Earth. With the searing sun constantly heating one side of the planet, rising warm air pushes rain clouds toward the twilight zone, which divides night into day. Here the moisture-laden clouds encounter dry, cold air

TRAPPIST-1e

TRAPPIST-1f

TRAPPIST-1g

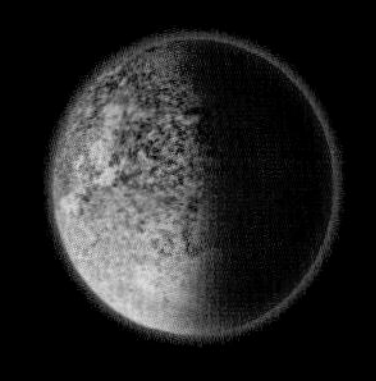
TRAPPIST-1h

flowing in from the frigid regions on the dark side. The meeting of these air masses creates havoc in the twilight zone. Falling snow turns to pelting rain, driven by fierce winds that erode surface rocks down to smooth, rounded shapes. The perpetual twilight in this transition zone, filled with salmon-colored clouds, is punctuated by lightning bolts blasting to the ground. As you traveled through the twilight region into the dark side, crystalline stars would gradually reveal themselves in the ever deepening blue-black sky. Here in the realm of eternal night, nearby planetary neighbors would cast reflected red light back onto the surface, creating a spooky, rosy-colored landscape.

Even though TRAPPIST-1e, -f, and -g orbit through the habitable zone together, each of these three worlds exhibits its own special characteristics. Nearest to its star, TRAPPIST-1e is a rocky world locked into a six-day orbit. Slightly smaller than Earth, its gravitational field is also reduced. If you weigh a hundred pounds on Earth, you'd weigh seventy-five pounds here. This is a warm world, with expansive deserts or oceans covering its sunny side. If there are oceans on TRAPPIST-1e, its atmosphere could be quite steamy and its sky filled with billowing, dark rain clouds. A strong gravitational interaction with its red dwarf sun could generate extreme volcanic activity and planetary quakes. A panorama filled with distant puffing volcanoes is possible here. From space, this world might appear Earthlike, but Earthlings wearing protective space suits might find it a lot more comfortable living on the dark side of the planet where cooler temperatures prevail.

TRAPPIST-1f is nearly the same size as Earth. Orbiting its sun in just 9.2 days, this planet has temperature ranges that could match those found in our atmosphere. Vast seas enriched by flowing rivers might ripple with pink shadows cast by passing cumulus clouds. We might find wide basins filled with algae-like plant life, nestled inside alien forests bordered by grassy savannas. On this planet, photosynthesis, adapted to the predominantly infrared light emanating from 1f's sun, would result in startling physical changes to plant life, creating green colors much darker than those on Earth. To our eyes, all plant life on TRAPPIST-1f would appear to be a deep, bizarre black.

Larger than its two neighbors, TRAPPIST-1g qualifies as a super-Earth. Its gravity would mirror Earth's, but we'd find chillier environmental conditions here more similar to those of Earth's polar regions or arctic conditions during the ice ages. Mountainous icebergs might drift across chunky oceans of floating ice, ringed by ice fields dotted with glacial lakes. This exoplanet's giant blazing sun would render the frozen wastelands blood-red as multiple planets larger than our full moon parade across the sky. Yes, TRAPPIST-1g would be a breathtaking and somewhat frightening world to see!

Before we leave these surreal alien exoplanets, let's take a moment to consider two important facts. There are possibly hundreds of millions of other Earthlike planets out there in our galaxy. *Check!* Approximately 80 percent of all the stars making up our Milky Way galaxy fall into the red dwarf category. *Check!* With this in mind, it's possible that the Earthlike planets found in the TRAPPIST-1 system represent what *most* other solar systems look like across the universe. So we have to ask ourselves: Could our sun and planetary neighbors be a space oddity? And just how unreal might life be out there on these ruby-colored alien worlds?

THE HOURGLASS NEBULA

MOST BEAUTIFUL OBJECT IN THE MILKY WAY

THERE IS AN overwhelming beauty to our universe that often surpasses words. It may be this fascination with mystery and beauty that draws so many people to astronomy. Across the vastness of space, images of colliding galaxies, exploding stars, and never-ending vistas lush with swirling clouds of vibrant colored gas and dust fill our minds with awe.

Images transmitted to Earth from space-based observatories like the Hubble Space Telescope present fleeting moments of captured time. The galaxies we see, the ever-increasing number of planets we monitor, and our sun, which spreads light at dawn and withdraws it at sunset—all seem to have been here forever. Mere Earthlings detect very few of the changes occurring in space over vast eons of time, though an occasional supernova may flare up for a few weeks or months, heralding a chaotic end to a distant star system. Whether we can see it or not, things do change.

Early stargazers scanning the heavens occasionally chanced upon small, spherical objects. Because of the round shapes of these objects, early sky observers like the great eighteenth-century British astronomer William Herschel thought they might be ghostly planets. He named them "planetary nebula." Centuries later, these spherical objects were properly identified as the spectral remains of former stars like our sun whose solar fires had burned out. Their stellar lives were over.

Of the remarkable planetary nebulae found in our skies, there is one that reigns above all the rest. The Hourglass Nebula, revered as the "Eye of God," displays a haunting celestial beauty. This is

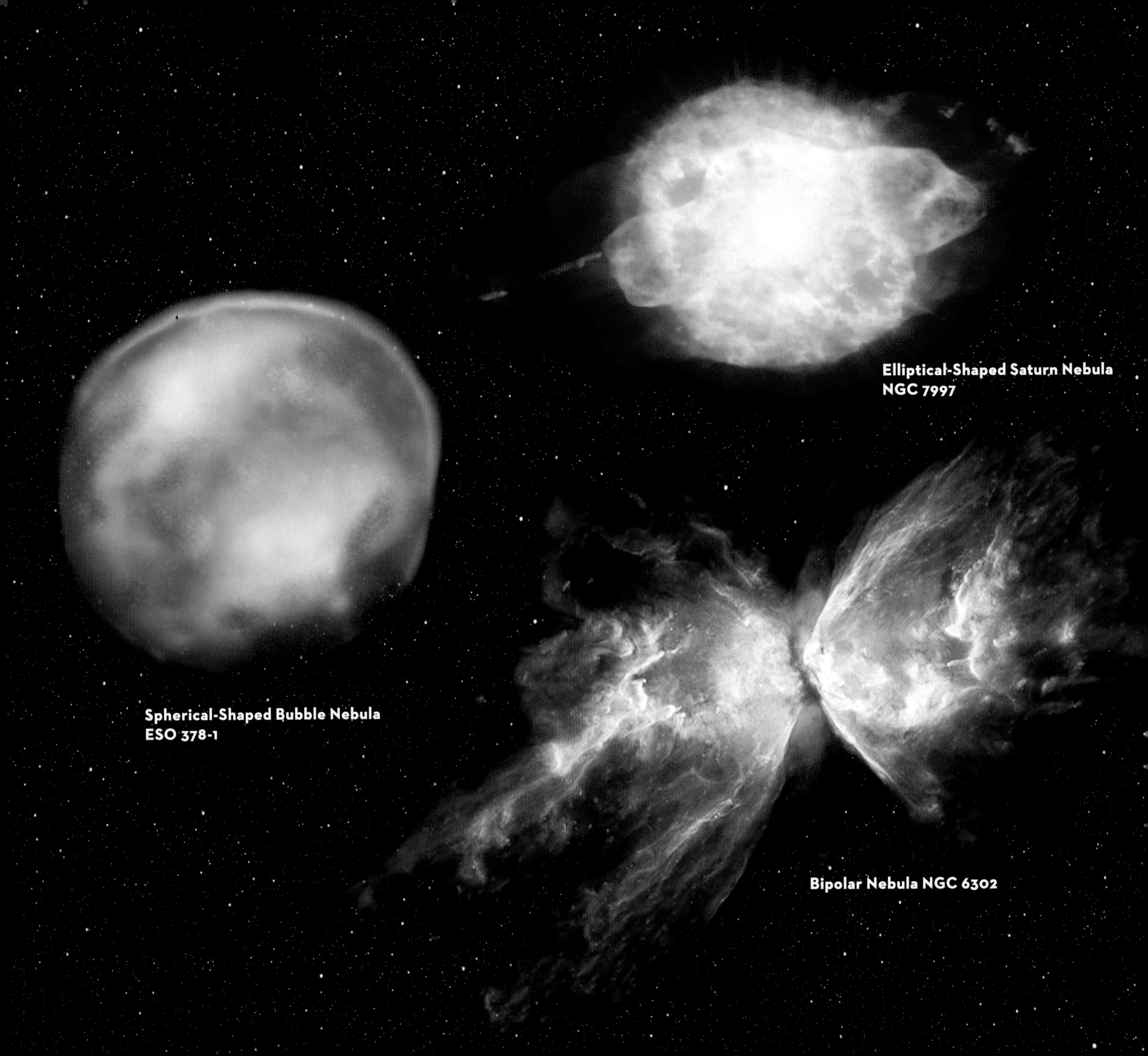
Elliptical-Shaped Saturn Nebula
NGC 7997
Spherical-Shaped Bubble Nebula
ESO 378-1
Bipolar Nebula NGC 6302

our sixth wonder of the Milky Way.

Planetary nebulae have been described as the "butterflies of space" because they exhibit so many different colors and varieties of shapes. It's estimated that some 10,000 planetary nebulae may exist throughout our Milky Way, but to date only 1,500 have been confirmed and categorized. The remaining ones may be concealed within immense clouds of dark gas and dust. As you can guess by now, there's a whole lot of gas and dust in our universe! Compared to stars and planets that exist for billions of years, planetary nebulae experience very short lifetimes that rarely exceed tens of thousands of years.

Planetary nebulae appear in three basic shapes: spherical ones that look like beach balls, elliptical egg-shaped ones, and bipolar ones that have two matching extended sides. The latter are the planetary nebulae that truly do resemble symmetrical butterflies. Scientists have yet to determine how these differing shapes are formed. Some may have been created when an old, dying star orbiting around another star was ripped apart by gravitational forces. Another theory is that rapidly spinning dying stars fling off puffy gas clouds, much like a hat might fly off your head on a fast merry-go-round. Now, think back to those dense groups of stars called globular clusters. Remember how we learned that the possibility of life depends upon the heavy metals formed by dying stars? Expanding planetary nebulae contain large amounts of these metals, as well as carbon, oxygen, and nitrogen atoms. These nebulae work as cosmic recyclers, churning gas and dust enriched with valuable heavy elements back into space. And big? Yessiree. Most planetary nebulae are about one light-year in diameter. Radiation from the central star of a planetary nebula can heat the surrounding gas to temperatures of up to 18,000° F (10,000° C), or almost twice the temperature of the surface of the sun. Those expanding gas shells really are hot, and that's why they glow with such brilliant colors!

The spectacular Hourglass Nebula is located eight thousand light-years from Earth, in the constellation Musca the Fly. (Yes, there is even a constellation out there honoring buzzing houseflies!) If we were to view the Hourglass Nebula tonight, the light we'd see actually left there some eight thousand years ago. That's several thousand years before humans invented writing or the wheel!

The Hourglass Nebula is classified as a bipolar, or two-sided, planetary nebula, although it does not appear this way from Earth due to the angle from which it's seen. (In case you're not familiar with an

Planetary nebulae are the ghosts of dying stars similar in size to our own sun. Someday, billions of years from now, our star will become a beautiful planetary nebula, too.

hourglass or sand timer, it's a measuring tool shaped like the number *8*, with a glass bulb at either end and a flat top and bottom. One bulb is filled with very fine sand. To measure time, you flip the full side up to the top, and when all the sand trickles down into the lower bulb, it signifies a certain time period has passed. You can flip an hourglass back and forth to measure time.) The Hourglass Nebula's peculiar rings echo the shape of an hourglass, and may have been created by separate bursts or bubbles of expanding stellar winds blowing out from a central white dwarf star. White dwarf stars are the remains of dying stars like our sun. They are highly compacted, shrunk down to about the size of Earth.

We have never seen anything quite like the Hourglass Nebula before. Astronomers know that the concentric red rings of this nebula originated from the outer gas layers of a dying red giant star, layers that contained large amounts of mixed nitrogen atoms and hydrogen atoms. The nebula's green colors are also mostly hydrogen atoms, the darker brown colors are carbon, and the famous blue and white of the Eye of God are rare forms of oxygen.

The Hourglass Nebula will not last forever. Now expanding at the rapid rate of several miles per second, its sands of time are quickly running out. As this nebula swells in size and its gases spread out, it grows fainter. There may not be more than a few thousand years left before it disappears completely from view. How lucky are we to have the opportunity to view this revered gem at this moment in time?

The Hourglass Nebula may be as beautiful as it is haunting, but it is also a glimpse into the future fate of our sun. At the end of our sun's lifetime, some five billion years from now, it will swell in size, becoming a red giant star that will extend well beyond the orbit of Venus—possibly reaching Earth. Burning through its original fuel supply, our sun will eventually eject its outer layers as an expanding bubble of gas into space. Left behind will be a newly formed white dwarf star, which will illuminate the expanding gas shell in a dazzling blue-green display, with tinges of red glowing gases. This will be the last goodbye from a star that harbored a remarkable solar system, one containing gas giants with stunning ring systems, frozen ice giants of emerald greens and blues, and small, rocky worlds—including one, covered by deep blue oceans, that gave birth to a remarkable species capable of standing upright and utilizing modern technologies. Like the Hourglass Nebula, our sun will become part of the fleeting cosmic butterfly menagerie of planetary nebulae that exist in the collection of stars we call the Milky Way galaxy.

"The Eye of God" feature in the core of this planetary nebula remains an oddity because of its haunting shape and magnificent colors.

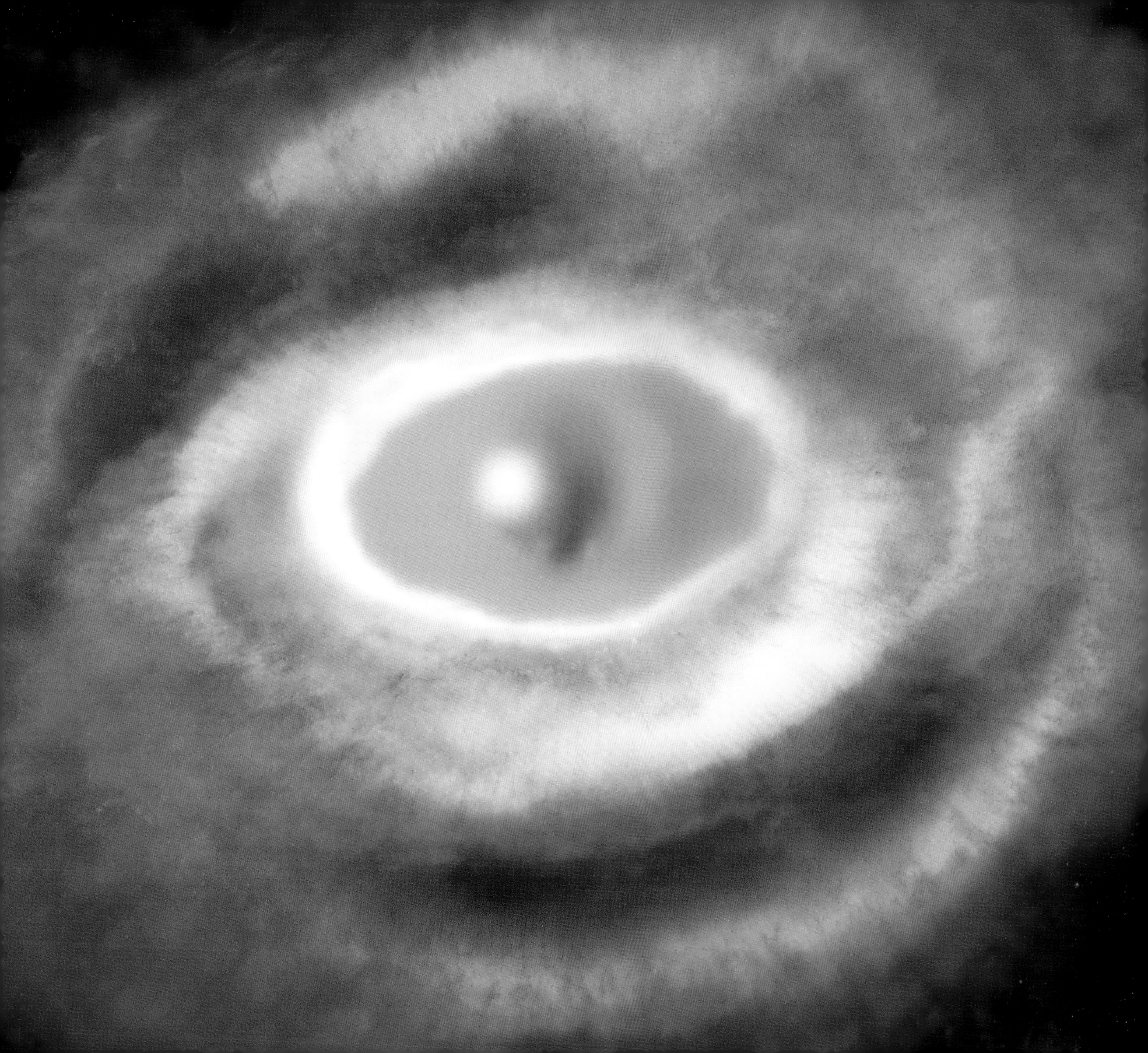

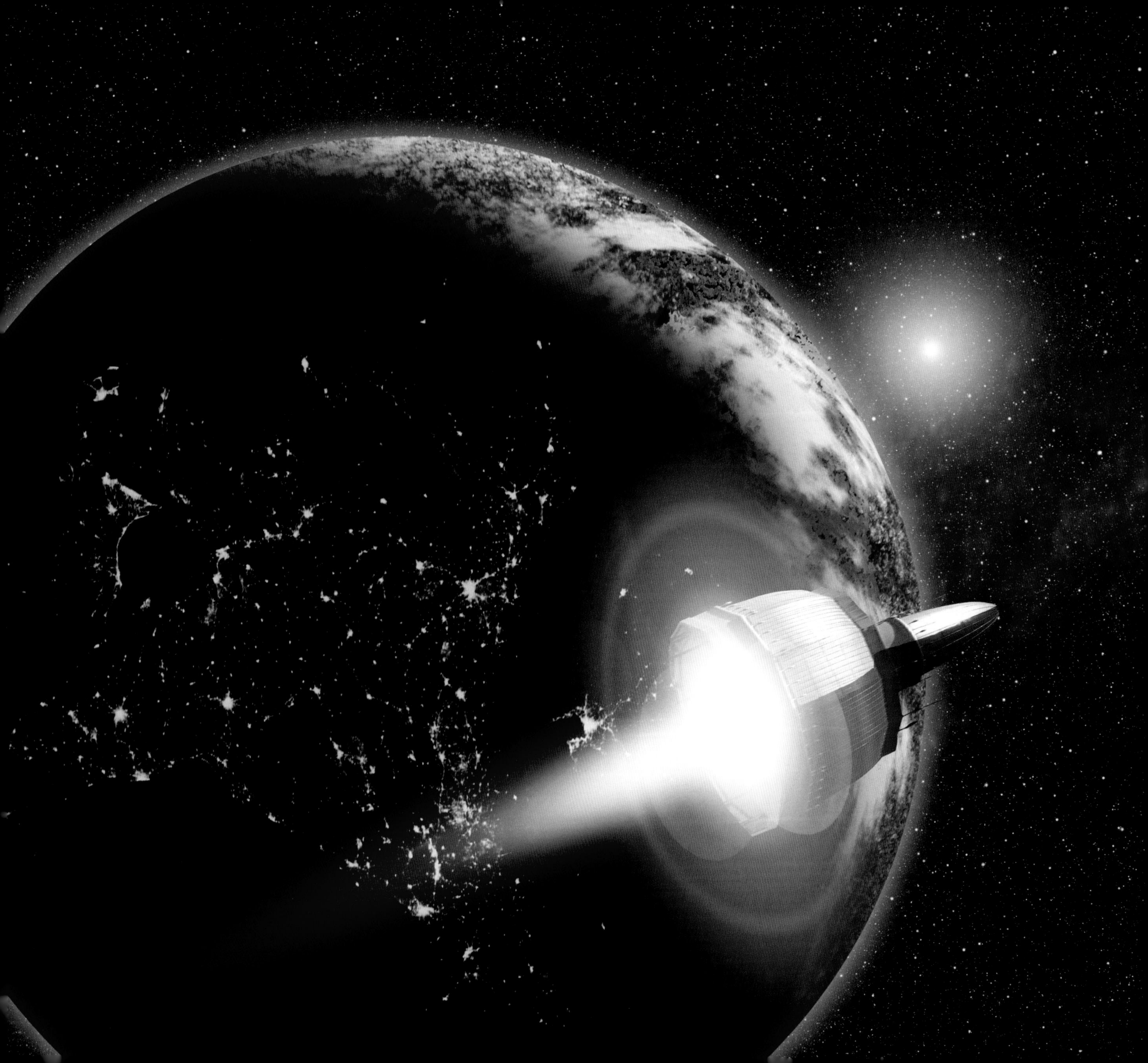

TABBY'S STAR

WEIRDEST OBJECT IN THE MILKY WAY

EVERYONE LOVES A good mystery—especially when it might involve space aliens! The idea that there may be intelligent life out there among the stars is not new. The Greeks, Romans, and Egyptians contemplated the possibility of extraterrestrial life one thousand years before the invention of the telescope. The sheer vastness of space forces us to accept the fact that we may not be alone. The prospect of finding life grows greater every day, considering there may be more than 8.8 billion habitable Earth-sized planets in the Milky Way. So, with all these big numbers, where are all the aliens? Today's popular culture is particularly fond of stories depicting alien armies invading Earth. People around the world continue to report unidentified flying objects hovering over cities and deserts at night. So the question remains: Do humans represent the most advanced form of life in the universe—or, more disconcerting, the *only* one? Scientists believe the concept of other life-forms existing beyond our solar system is reasonable. But how will we ever know?

In September 2015, a team of astronomers led by Yale astronomer Tabetha Boyajian announced the discovery of star KIC 8462852, at a distance of about 1,300 light-years from Earth. Boyajian and her team observed an erratic pattern: KIC 8462852 seemed to be dimming, or losing its light, in a way never seen before. Nicknamed "Tabby's Star" after Tabetha, the discovery made headline news around the world. Could something be occurring around this distant star that might involve alien life? Let's explore these controversial ideas as we investigate Tabby's Star, our seventh wonder of the Milky Way galaxy.

The first attempt to locate life in the Milky Way was made by Cornell University astronomer Frank Drake in 1960, when he pointed an 85-foot (26 m) radio telescope toward two nearby stars. He listened for any radio signals coming from the planets that might be orbiting around the sun-like star Tau Ceti, twelve light-years away. No alien messages or broadcasts were picked up—Zero. Zip. *Nada*. To this day, researchers continue to point oversize radio dishes toward the millions of stars in our galaxy, hoping to intercept a signal, or at least a tweet! Nothing looked promising until 2007, when astronomers

(ABOVE) Frank Drake. (RIGHT) The Howard E. Tatel Radio Telescope in Green Bank, West Virginia, was used by Frank Drake in the first search for extraterrestrial intelligences in the universe.

pinpointed a number of mysterious blasts of radio waves emanating from a distant dwarf galaxy some three billion light-years beyond the Milky Way. They were named "fast radio bursts," or FRBs, because they lasted for just a moment. Flashing across space at one-thousandth of a second, FRBs are one of the most baffling astronomical puzzles yet. Except for one hardy repeating signal, the rest of the bursts seem to come from different sources. This led scientists to wonder: Are FRBs actually ancient cosmic messages sent billions of years ago? Are they a type of "We are here!" signal from groups of advanced alien civilizations, or the product of yet another new exotic object out there in space?

These bursts remain a huge mystery. When we explore how we might initiate galactic contact, broadcasting a series of FRBs from Earth makes sense. If we sent out short, powerful radio bursts, much like a lighthouse sending out beacons of light, someone or something out there in the cosmos might pick up our signal and respond. So listening, watching, and waiting for replies to our dispatches may yield findings of other life-forms. But are there any other ways that we could point to the existence of alien civilizations in space? The initial discovery of Tabby's Star raised that exciting possibility. Ah, the starry plot thickens!

We've learned that measuring dips in light coming from a star can be useful in detecting planets. If you train a telescope on a star and record any tiny changes of light as a planet passes across the face of the star, you may have just bagged a new planet. This is known as the transit method, and it has led to a bounty of planetary discoveries. Thousands of new distant worlds have been cataloged this way. When astronomers using NASA's planet-hunting Kepler space telescope looked at the star KIC 8462852, they found that it dimmed in ways not typically associated with the transit of planets. In one instance, 22 percent of Tabby's light was suddenly blocked out. Something big must have passed in front of this star to explain this massive drop in light. One hypothesis, or proposed explanation, was that a swarm of irregular-size comets were orbiting the star, or that a large, Saturn-like ring surrounding the star was breaking apart. As time and gravity drew the comets or ring fragments toward the star, they would end up crashing onto the surface. If this were the case, Tabby's Star should be brightening as the dust and rocks disintegrate. Instead, another startling discovery came to light when astronomers examined the old glass photographic plates Annie Jump Cannon had worked with. Tabby's Star had actually been dimming for the past one hundred

years or more, and darkening quite dramatically over the past three years. These were not comets orbiting Tabby's Star. Something else must be happening here.

Meanwhile, back in the corridors of science departments, another strange hypothesis was circulating. What if a passing black hole was causing the dimming of Tabby's Star? This explanation was quickly dismissed when astronomers realized that the gravitational field from a passing black hole would also distort background stars. No surrounding stars were being warped, so the dimming effect didn't seem to be the result of a passing black hole.

Now the wildest of all speculations was considered. Could the continuous dimming of Tabby's Star be caused by aliens constructing a superstructure around the star to capture the full energy of their sun and beam it back to a home world? Holy moly, could this be real? In 1964, Soviet astronomer Nikolai Kardashev proposed there might be three different types of advanced civilizations existing in the universe, separated by billions of years of evolution. A Type I civilization would use all the energy collected from their home planet to power their technologies. Someday, when we tap into the molten core of the Earth to produce all the steam and electrical power we need, we will be considered a Type I society. A Type II civilization would capture all the energy from their sun to power their technologies. A Type III civilization would harness all the available energy from their galaxy. Could the dimming of Tabby's Star be the result of a Type II civilization busily constructing something called a Dyson sphere around their sun? A Dyson sphere is an engineering concept developed back in the 1960s by famed physicist Freeman Dyson. An advanced civilization capable of building a structure around their star should be able to capture all the energy that typically radiates away into space. This massive force of solar power could run a lot of electric cars, Xboxes, and spaceships! Thousands of years from now, this is a project Earthlings could undertake to

A Dyson sphere is a hypothetical megastructure that completely encompasses a star to capture most or all of its power output. This was once a theory applied to Tabby's Star, but has now been disproved.

harness all the energy radiating out from our sun. (Finally, the Earth would truly run on clean energy!)

So we were left with yet another huge puzzle. What was causing Tabby's Star to dim over time, and exactly what was crossing in front of it? Could it be giant sunspots? To make the light dip this much, those sunspots would have to be a hundred times larger than any sunspot we've ever recorded on our own sun. This is unimaginable. Could it be the remains of two planets that have just crashed together? This sounds possible, but why then does the dimming just keep increasing over time? As the gravity of the star pulls the debris onto its surface, Tabby's light should be growing brighter. If none of these hypotheses explain what we are observing, then what we are left with is perplexing. Is it possible we've stumbled upon an alien home-improvement project to upgrade their power grid? Sadly, the apparent answer is no. No alien ETs found here. The most mysterious star in the Milky Way appears to be shrouded by a lumpy stellar ring of gas and dust. Still, the discovery of why KIC 8462852 is dimming presents a perfect example of how good science works. A mysterious phenomenon is observed, a hypothesis or idea about its cause is put forward, and then research is conducted to confirm or reject the idea. Tabby's Star may not harbor an advanced alien civilization in the process of constructing a Dyson sphere, but someday, another remote discovery may confirm we are not alone. For today, Tabby's Star remains quite a wonder in our Milky Way galaxy.

What the hypothetical dust ring orbiting Tabby's Star 1,300 light-years away from Earth might look like.

Astronomers have discovered a large, deep magenta-colored planet about fifty-seven light-years away from Earth. This "Pink Planet" is still glowing from the heat of its formation.

OTHER WONDERS TO WONDER ABOUT

WAY BACK IN the sixteenth century, a new novelty appeared in many wealthier homes throughout Europe, meant to assert a sense of sophistication and worldliness. It was known as a "cabinet of curiosities." ("Cabinet" at that time could also be a "wonder room," not just a fancy piece of furniture.) Inside were neatly displayed artifacts collected from around the world—for example, a pressed flower from India, a fossilized shark tooth from Great Britain, the skeleton of a reptile, a beautifully mounted azure butterfly from the Amazon, a religious relic from Rome, or a small classical statue from ancient Greece.

For astronomers, the Milky Way represents such a cabinet, brimming with treasures and glorious curiosities. Narrowing the list of our galaxy's wonders down to the few final choices included in this book was quite challenging. I began with a long list because there is still so much to consider out there in the Milky Way. A few other astonishingly curious objects warrant a shout-out.

Fifty-seven light-years away, circling a star much like our sun, is a gas giant planet that is so hot, it appears magenta in color. Named "Pink Planet," by its discoverers, GJ 504b is a young world, still glowing from the heat generated by its formation. Broiling at a temperature of 460° F (237° C), it would be a deadly place to call home, but it certainly would be lovely to look at.

While the surface temperature of Pink Planet is hot enough to melt lead, WASP-12b wins the prize for hottest known planet in our galaxy. Measuring a killer 2,800° F (1,538° C), WASP-12b may also be the most short-lived planet out there. Because it orbits so close to its parent star, it is slowly being pulled in and may only have a few million years left before it is completely devoured by its sun.

In Greek mythology, the Pleiades were seven lovely sisters, daughters of Atlas and his wife, Pleione. To

stargazers, they are known as an open star cluster in the constellation Taurus the Bull. In photographs, the Pleiades resemble a small dipper surrounded by a stunning cobalt-blue reflection nebula. These stars are so young and so new that their nuclear fires had not yet turned on when the first dinosaurs lumbered about the Earth. If you looked up into the sky seventy-five million years ago, the Pleiades wouldn't have been there.

Another on my list is Achernar, the ninth-brightest star in the heavens. Due to its rapid rotation, it has the flattest shape of any star known in the Milky Way galaxy. This egg-shaped wonder is spinning at a dizzying rate of 155 miles (250 km) per second. As it rotates, Achernar throws out trails of gas thousands of times faster than a normal star like our sun does, leaving behind two oddly twisted tails.

The "Pillars of Creation" is one of the most famous images ever captured by the Hubble Space Telescope. Located seven thousand light-years away, these enormous elephant trunks of interstellar gas and dust were intact when their light left there seven thousand years ago. But today, these pillars may have already disappeared. Astronomers know that around six thousand years ago, a deadly blast wave from a nearby supernova likely crashed into them like a tidal wave, possibly washing the pillars away. Again, this reinforces what we learned earlier. Everything we see in space is the way it appeared in the past and not the way it may actually look today.

Lastly, the great Crab Nebula, located in the constellation Taurus the Bull, is what remains of a supernova that lit up our night skies in 1054. It's called the Crab Nebula because early astronomers thought it looked like a little crustacean crawling around at the beach. Appearing six times brighter than the planet Venus, this supernova was visible at night for two years and in the daytime sky for twenty-three days. Chinese astronomers labeled it a "guest star," something new that suddenly appeared in the night skies. The Crab Nebula contains a tiny neutron star only a few miles in diameter that spins thirty times a second. The neutrons inside this star are jammed so close together, one teaspoon would weigh more than thirty thousand aircraft carriers put together. Mega-astonishing, but true!

All these potential marvels were considered for the top seven list in this book. Although they were not included they do remain marvels just the same. Expanding this search beyond the Milky Way, one ponders: What other wonders might exist out there in this vast universe?

This illustration of the "Pillars of Creation" is based on images from the Hubble Space Telescope. The trunk-shaped columns of interstellar gas and dust are in the Eagle Nebula some 6,500 to 7,000 light-years away from Earth.

BEYOND THE MILKY WAY

WE LIVE ON a planet spinning on its axis at a speed of 1,000 miles (1,600 km) per hour, traveling a yearly trek around the sun at 66,600 miles (107,200 km) per hour. So it's true: We're definitely livin' in the fast lane! The Earth is located in an area called the Orion Spur, in an arm of the Milky Way galaxy. Our entire solar system travels on average at a rate of 515,000 miles (828,000 km) per hour in its 230- to 250-million-year journey around our galaxy to complete one cosmic year. The Milky Way is not static either. It travels through space as the universe continues to expand and accelerate. Everything is in motion. This concept is enough to make any Earthling's head spin. As we make our way through the cosmos, ever greater mysteries and wonders abound. Here's one: At a distance of 225 million light-years away from us, the biggest known black hole in the universe is nestled in the center of the distant galaxy NGC 1277. This black hole is billions of times more massive than our sun. Shall we make a stop? I don't think so! Here's another: Located nearly a billion light-years away is the largest known galaxy in the universe. Shaped like a gargantuan egg, it contains one hundred trillion stars and measures an incredible six million light-years in diameter! In comparison, our Milky Way galaxy measures approximately 160,000 light-years in diameter.

Other bizarre conditions that rattle the mind exist beyond our galaxy. The universe is full of dark energy. It is an unidentified force that is speeding up the acceleration of stars and galaxies throughout the universe. Combined, dark matter and dark energy make up a whopping 95 percent of the universe. That's right. All the stars, planets, moons, gas clouds, and galaxies that appear in the images taken by the Hubble Space Telescope constitute less than 5 percent of our universe. The rest, it would seem, is still unknown.

The universe surrounding our small blue planet—a world orbiting around a medium-size yellow star, itself orbiting inside a large spiral galaxy that is part of a larger group of galaxies all traveling through space—can inspire absolute disbelief. The next time you have the opportunity to look out at the stars on a clear night, take a moment to realize how special you are, Earthling. We represent the only life in the 4.5-billion-year history of this planet that has had the curiosity and the capability to search beyond our own world and probe the mysteries of the universe. We are the only species to have ever sent robotic spacecraft to explore our solar system and dream of traveling to the stars. Now that's what I call intelligent life!

UNDER THE STARS

AS A YOUNG READER, I marveled at the fantastic and often surreal photographs of outer space that were taken at big observatories like Kitt Peak in Arizona or Palomar in California, where the 200-inch (508-cm) telescope was so large you could actually sit inside it! As a young budding scientist, I dreamed of having my own telescope to explore the skies from my backyard. In middle school, I embarked on my own journey to the stars. Discovering books in my local library on telescope making, I learned how to grind and polish glass telescope mirrors, fasten them inside cardboard tubes, and then assemble plumbers' pipe fittings to construct a mount to support and point my telescope. It wasn't perfect, but it worked! From the end of my driveway, I soared through the solar system, viewing craters on the moon, the polar ice caps on Mars, the rings of Saturn, and the moons of Jupiter. Venturing out beyond the planets into the Milky Way was even more breathtaking. There were just so many stars out there! In summertime, the bright star Albireo, at the head of Cygnus the Swan, became two stars in my eyepiece—one blazing golden yellow and the other a brilliant blue. As I swept my telescope across the constellation Lyra the Harp, the Ring Nebula suddenly popped into view. Looking like a small cosmic smoke ring, it was the remains of a distant star like our own sun that is now a planetary nebula.

Although there are so many spectacular images taken by the Hubble Space Telescope and other marvelous instruments, I still

telescope in my personal observatory, located high up in the Rocky Mountains in southern Colorado. On a breathtakingly clear, dark night, I can traverse the heart of the Milky Way, viewing toward the southern constellation Sagittarius the Archer. In winter, with snow blanketing the ground, you will find me exploring the turbulent clouds of gas and dust that make up the stellar nursery of the Great Nebula in Orion. Yes, after all these years, I still enjoy getting lost in the heavens. Pictures online, on TV, or in books are not enough for me. This personal connection allows me to imagine what it must be like "out there" when I write about or paint alien planets that no Earthling may ever see. It's through my own imagination that I experience the splendor of our Milky Way galaxy, with all its mysteries that remain hidden light-years beyond reach. If you, young reader, have not yet had the opportunity to see the heavens through a telescope, I encourage you to start now. Today there are many bargain telescopes on the market that would make great starter scopes. There may also be a local astronomy club in your area that hosts star parties, or perhaps someone at your school or local library has a telescope. Ask around and you may be pleasantly surprised. If you are ready to explore the universe at the speed of light and travel through space and time into the unknown, some of the grandest adventures of all await you. Our mystical universe calls out with ancient magical voices. Listen closely and you too may be lucky enough to hear them.

KEEP EXPLORING!

BOOKS

Aguilar, David A. *13 Planets: The Latest View of the Solar System*. Washington, DC: National Geographic, 2011.

——. *Alien Worlds: Your Guide to Extraterrestrial Life*. Washington, DC: National Geographic, 2013.

——. *Cosmic Catastrophes: Seven Ways to Destroy a Planet Like Earth*. New York: Viking/Smithsonian, 2016.

——. *Seven Wonders of the Solar System*. New York: Viking/Smithsonian, 2017.

——. *Space Encyclopedia: A Tour of Our Solar System and Beyond*. Washington, DC: National Geographic, 2013.

——. *Super Stars: The Biggest, Hottest, Brightest, Most Explosive Stars in the Milky Way*. Washington, DC: National Geographic, 2010.

Maran, Stephen P. *Astronomy for Dummies*. Hoboken, NJ: John Wiley & Sons, Inc., 2017.

MEDIA

NASA's Unexplained Files (Season 5), Science Channel
sciencechannel.com/tv-shows/nasas-unexplained-files/

"Alien Faces," *Our Universe*, The History Channel
youtube.com/watch?v=3cuZVYWw600

WEBSITES

David A. Aguilar author site
davidaguilar.org

NASA/Astronomy Picture of the Day (APOD)
apod.nasa.gov/apod/astropix.html

Smithsonian National Air and Space Museum
nasm.si.edu

Space.com
space.com/science-astronomy

MUSIC

Here is some of the music I listened
to while painting the images for this book.

Alpha Wave Movement: *Cosmology* and *A Distant Signal*
Constance Demby: *Sanctum Sanctorum*
Jonn Serrie: *And the Stars Go with You*
James Wild: *Goodbye Earth Hello Cosmos*

ACKNOWLEDGMENTS

THE FIRST PERSONS I wish to thank are my agents, Brenda Bowen and Dan Mandel, who presented me with the opportunity to write and illustrate my three latest books, *Cosmic Catastrophes, Seven Wonders of the Solar System,* and *Seven Wonders of the Milky Way.* This adventure would not have left Earth's orbit without their generous support. The next person I wish to convey my deepest gratitude to is my editor, Sheila Keenan, whose wit, style, and pithy questions continually kept me on track. I also love the way she always ends her emails with "Onward!" In laying out the visual appearance of this book, special thanks must go to Jim Hoover, who exceeded all expectations. And thanks also to my diligent, eagle-eyed copyeditors, Ryan Sullivan and Janel Pascal.

I also owe a great debt of recognition to two dear friends and scientific colleagues who gave much of their time in helping clarify various concepts and ideas presented in this book. Stellar applause goes out to author and renowned astronomer Stephen P. Maran and the amazing Christine Pulliam of the Hubble Space Telescope Institute. Without their input, thoughts, and ideas, this book would not be what it is today.

Every book begins as a long journey that weaves through time taking a lot of roads less traveled before reaching its destination. Twenty years ago, the genesis of this book materialized over excited conversations with two dear friends, Randall Moke and Bob Amend, sitting outside our favorite restaurant on the Pearl Street Mall in Boulder, Colorado. Two decades later, those wild ideas reached a successful liftoff!

Most of all, this book is dedicated with love to my wife, Ms. ASTRID, who is still my girlfriend, color commentator, and inspirational muse after all these years together. Words cannot capture the sheer enjoyment when two creative minds, working together, make dreams of the universe become reality.

Lastly, this book is dedicated to you, young reader. I envy you the astounding wonders of the cosmos that will be revealed in your lifetime. Is there life out there? Are there other universes out there? Who let the dogs out? In the coming years, you will know the answers to all these questions. I hope this book is one small step in your long journey of discovery aboard this tiny blue world we call home.

– D. A. A.

Note: Page numbers in *italics* refer to illustrations.

Achernar star, 73

Big Bang, 25
black holes, 10, 38, 67, 75

Crab Nebula, 73

dark energy, 14, 75
dark matter, 10, 14, 75
Dyson spheres, *66*, 67

Earth, 42–43, 50, 74
Earthlike planets, 13, 49–50, 52–53, 55
exoplanets, 41–42, 44
Eye of God, 57, 60, *61*

fast radio bursts (FRBs), 65

galaxies, 9, 25
globular clusters, *24*, 25–31, *27, 28, 30–31,* 59
Great Nebula in Orion (M42), 16–23
    colors of, *18,* 20, *21*
    life cycle of, 22
    star formation in, 19, 20

Hourglass Nebula, 56–61
    and Eye of God, 57, 60, *61*
    shape of, *56,* 59–60
Hubble Space Telescope
    and known universe, 57, 75
    and Pillars of Creation, *72,* 73
    and stars in globular clusters, 29
    views of protostars (proplyds), 20

J1407b, *40,* 41–47
    moons of, *44–45,* 45, 47
    rings of, 42, *44–45,* 44–45, 47

Jupiter, 42, *43*, 45

life on other planets
    on Earthlike planets, 13, 50, 55
    and fast radio bursts (FRBs), 65
    in globular clusters, 31
    and heavy metals, 29, 31, 59
    intelligent, 63, 67
    on planet-sized moons, 47
    plant life and photosynthesis, 55
    and red dwarf stars, 13, 50, 55
    search for, 13-15, *14–15*, *64*, 64–65

metals, heavy, 29, *30–31*, 31
Milky Way
    black hole of, 10
    distances to objects in, 10, *11*
    formation of, 9, 25
    glow of, *9*, 9–10
    shape of, *8*, 9
    sun's orbit around, 10
moons, 44, *44–45*, 45, 47

OBAFGKM classification system of stars, 34–35, *35*
Omega Centauri, 24–31
    light-years to, *11*
    and search for life, 29
    star field visible from inside, *30–31*, 31
    visibility of, 25, 26, *27,* 29

Pillars of Creation, *72*, 73
Pink Planet (GJ 504b), *70*, 71
planetary nebula, 57, *58*, 59
planets, newly formed, 20
Pleiades, 71, 73

radio telescopes, *64*, 64–65

red dwarf stars, 13, 50, 52–53, 55
red giants, 35–36

solar systems, genesis of, 20
solar winds, 20
speed of light, 13
sun, *12*
    distance to, *11*
    life cycle of, 60
    orbit around the Milky Way, 10
    size of, 13, 33, *37*
    yellow G classification of, 33

Tabby's Star, 62–69
    dimming of, 65, 67–68
    name of, 62–63
    rings of, 68, *69*
telescopes
    access to, 77
    and "lookback time," *10*
    and search for life, 13–15, *14–15*
    See also Hubble Space Telescope
tidal locking, 50, *51*, 52–53
TRAPPIST-1 (red dwarf), 49–55
    Earthlike planets of, 50–55, *52–53, 54–55*
    as red dwarf star, 50, 52
    size of, *13*

UY Scuti, 32–39
    collapse of, 38
    distance to, 36
    red hypergiant classification of, 35
    size of, 33, 36, *37*

Vega, 33, 36, *37*

523.113 AGU
7124